R. Spencer

A Survey of the History, Commerce, and Manufactures of Lancashire

R. Spencer

A Survey of the History, Commerce, and Manufactures of Lancashire

ISBN/EAN: 9783744726467

Printed in Europe, USA, Canada, Australia, Japan

Cover: Foto ©ninafisch / pixelio.de

More available books at **www.hansebooks.com**

A SURVEY

OF THE

HISTORY, COMMERCE AND MANUFACTURES

OF

LANCASHIRE

TOGETHER WITH

EXTRACTS, REPRODUCED BY REQUEST,

FROM

"THE HOME TRADE OF MANCHESTER"

AND

A BIOGRAPHICAL SKETCH

OF

REUBEN SPENCER, Esq., J.P.

INCLUDING

JUBILEE DEMONSTRATIONS

———•——

LONDON

THE BIOGRAPHICAL PUBLISHING COMPANY

1897

LANCASHIRE.

"I Speak but in the Figures and Comparisons of it."—*Shakespeare*
(Henry V., act iv. sc. vii.).

IN attempting to briefly outline the position and importance at the present day of that most interesting and notable of English shires, the County Palatine of Lancaster, it must be our endeavour in these few introductory pages not so much to essay the difficult task of a concise historical review as to call special attention to those epochs and achievements of Lancastrian annals in which the genius of the people of this county has been more particularly displayed. At the same time it will be consistent with the scope of such a work as this to speak in some detail of the natural resources of the county itself, which have enabled Lancashire men in general to find a congenial and profitable field for the exercise of their well-known practical talents and progressive spirit. It is a rather remarkable fact that, rich as it is in associations of the past, and closely as it has been connected with many of the most stirring events of our national history, Lancashire life should in modern times have betaken itself to a channel quite at variance with the romantic tendency of its early records. In this circumstance we have the keynote to the character of the Lancastrian people, to whom activity and movement are essentials of daily existence, and who neither could nor would subsist upon the bread of idleness. In the old days of unenlightenment (if we may use the word), when Science was groping her way through the gloom of ignorance to the great day of knowledge and discovery, and when all the useful arts were either in a primitive condition or in a state of gradual transition, the men of Lancashire began to lay the foundations of their county's prosperity; and as the years passed on, by continuous exercise of those faculties of foresight and shrewd perception which their descendants still possess in such a marked degree, they strengthened the position they had taken up, and made for themselves a name in the world of industry the renown of which has not ceased to increase down to the present hour. They thought constantly of the future, too, and foresaw possibilities which have been realised to the fullest extent in later times. What they did and what their successors have since done in many new directions has given us the Lancashire of to-day—the "workshop of the world," and England's premier county in wealth, population, and magnitude of business undertakings.

Within the borders of Lancashire, as we know it now, stand some of the largest and busiest towns in the British Isles, including the second port of the Empire, and the wonderful metropolis of the cotton trade. Within the same boundaries there dwells a vast population, the individual units of which are trained by daily practice and ever-present example in habits of thrift and industry, and the great majority of whom continue to exhibit in a striking degree those powers of energy and that aptitude in the organisation and administration of large undertakings which have made the name of Lancashire a synonym for all that is expert and enterprising in commercial effort. Genius has manifested itself in this favoured county in many walks of life other than that of business. Art has flourished in Lancashire, and found munificent supporters and patrons among the merchant princes of the county. Literature and poetry, science and invention, have all fared well in this land of industry, and the great natural talent of Lancastrians in music is well known. In the arduous labour of mechanical advancement and improvement no English county has shone more brilliantly than Lancashire; such names as those of Hargreaves, Arkwright, Crompton, and Cartwright shed lustre upon the industrial history of the whole nation. The educational resources of Lancashire are as complete as an inborn love of knowledge can make them ; and the social and general condition of the many thriving boroughs, towns, and cities that attract the attention of the traveller in this part of England reveals a special talent for the promotion of communal interests and the management of municipal affairs. Thus, in manifold aspects, does Lancashire present a subject full of interest to the historian, the biographer, and the student of those events which bear upon local and national welfare ; and in some of its varied features having a special relationship to the life and work of its leading men, we may here briefly consider this important division of the Kingdom. In the first place a few remarks concerning the history of the county are almost indispensable in such a sketch as this, and they may be appropriately introduced here before we proceed further.

Of all the divisions of England there is none that has a stronger claim to be regarded as a county of to-day than Lancashire. The spirit of modern energy and progress is so universally manifest here, and all the busy centres of trade and population partake of it so largely in the whole routine of their daily life, that it becomes difficult to carry the mind back to a period when Lancashire possessed few or none of those attributes which constitute the basis of her greatness at the present day. True, she has always had her indomitable people and her wealth of natural resources, but even a clever people may be improved and educated, and the richest of nature's treasures may lie hidden for ages pending the advent of the discoverer and the processes of development that follow in his train. Time was when the men of Lancashire had little opportunity for the exercise of their higher talents, and when the mineral wealth of their county lay all unused, if not actually unknown. Wholly occupied, as he is, in maintaining his forward position in the "fierce competition of the important and imperative present," the average Lancastrian of to-day has little inclination and less time to trouble himself about the condition of his native county in ages gone by. The fact remains, nevertheless, that Lancashire has had a most interesting past, and the details of its early history point to a very fascinating field for the researches of the archæologist, all the more fascinating, perhaps, because much of the remote record of the county is very obscure.

Another notable point is the scarcity of what are variously known as "ancient monuments" and "relics of the past." Even that indefatigable antiquarian, William Camden, writing in the Elizabethan period, was forced to say that he could not make much out of the vague ruins then existing in Lancashire; and of these very few indeed are now traceable. All this might seem to point to a very high antiquity indeed for this county, but at the very outset we are confronted with a "poser," so to speak, in the fact that no mention of Lancashire occurs either in the old Saxon Chronicles or in the record of the Domesday Survey. However, the labours of able and zealous historians, and the researches of the many scientific and other societies that adorn the intellectual side of Lancashire life, have done much to pierce the gloom that envelops the early periods of local history in this quarter of the Kingdom, and have enabled us to place confidence in some important and well-supported evidences. For instance, it is certain enough that a portion of Lancashire was occupied in pre-Christian times by a section of that powerful and warlike tribe of Britons known as the Brigantes, who are famous for their dauntless and uncompromising resistance of the Roman invasion, and for their long-continued refusal to submit to conquest by the legions of the Cæsars. Eventually, however, after many a fierce conflict, these remote ancestors of the sturdy Lancastrian stock were forced to give up the unequal contest, and to yield to the might and strategy of Agricola and his disciplined troops. Then did eastern and north-eastern Lancashire become a part of the Roman province of Maxima Cæsariensis.

For several centuries subsequent to this the mist of obscurity hangs heavily over Lancashire, and it is not until we approach the Saxon period that a little more light is obtained. There are evidences to show that, just as they refused to acknowledge the Romans, so the people of Lancashire would have none of the Saxon conquest, and they made a brave fight of it, until about the year 680 A.D., when King Egfrid finally vanquished them, and incorporated their territory in the kingdom of Northumbria, which Ida had founded a hundred and thirty-three years previously. Doubtless there was progress of a kind under the Saxon rule. The great fact of that period was the establishment of Christianity upon a firm footing in Britain, and this implies a degree of moral advancement which could not be without beneficial effect upon the general life of the people. The Saxons also encouraged the mechanical arts and fostered learning, but these pursuits of peace must have been sorely interrupted by the ruthless and repeated incursions of the predatory and piratical Norsemen, who literally made life "not worth living" along the coasts of Britain in the tenth century. The short period of absolute Danish rule in this country, and the turbulence of the brief era of the Saxon restoration, produced no other effect than that of the reduction of England to a state of desperate chaos. As Baines, the historian of Lancashire, pointedly remarks: "Pierced by barbarian hordes, torn by internal divisions, and ruled by foreign masters, the country was for a long time like a seething cauldron, and the scene of overwhelming and crushing calamity."

In this condition did William the Conqueror find England when, after he had dealt the death-blow to the Saxon Heptarchy on the fateful field of Hastings, he marched northward to subjugate a people who had not for many a year had a clear and definite idea as to who was or was not their rightful lord and sovereign. The energy with which he accomplished this work is well known to the student of history, and in the fulness of time the various administrative divisions of England were parcelled out among puissant Norman barons, who claimed the right of participation in the spoils of conquest. Lancashire was doubtless treated in this manner, and after the lapse of years we hear of it coming under the domination of Roger de Poictou, who was lord of Lancaster until the reign of Edward I., when he appears to have incurred the royal displeasure, and the penalty of banishment in consequence. The title, Earl of Lancaster, appears to have first been borne by a member of the reigning house in 1267, when Henry III. bestowed it upon his youngest son, Edmund Crouchback. The family of Edmund retained the title for nearly a hundred years, and in 1353 Henry Plantagenet, a member of that family and a descendant of Edmund, became Duke of Lancaster. His son-in-law, John of Gaunt, succeeded him in 1361. John was the fourth son of Edward III., and for his benefit that monarch elevated Lancashire to the dignity of a County Palatine in 1376. Henry, Earl of Hereford, and son of John of Gaunt, succeeded to the Palatine dukedom in due course, and as he became King (under the title of Henry IV.) on the deposition of Richard II. in 1399, the Duchy of Lancaster then became merged in the Crown, and since that time it has been usual for the reigning sovereign to bear the title. The land revenues of the Crown are much enriched by the Duchy of Lancaster. At the time of the Queen's accession the revenues of the Duchy, after deducting all expenses, amounted to about £30,000 per annum, and the payment to Her Majesty at that period was £12,000. Since then they have increased very considerably, amounting in 1890 to £88,988 net, and the payment to Her Majesty at this latter period was £50,000. The present Chancellor of the Duchy of Lancaster is the Right Hon. Lord James of Hereford.

From this brief statistical divergence we may now return to the thread of Lancastrian history in the Middle Ages, when much disorder prevailed throughout the county, chiefly in consequence of the frequent incursions of the Scots, who, during the time of Robert Bruce, often carried their depredations as far south as Preston. Later on, in the time of Henry VII., the cause of the pretender, Lambert Simnel, was supported here, and a great assembly of forces took place in the Furness district, under the Earl of Lincoln and Lord Lovel; who, with the assistance of the local abbots and some of the influential families of this neighbourhood, sought to advance the claims of Simnel to the throne. The somewhat ignominious ending of this movement, and the eventual retirement of Simnel into the obscurity of a royal menial, are too well known to need recalling. Presently came the great crash of the Reformation, bringing with it the complete *bouleversement* of religious affairs and authority, and immediately Lancashire was again plunged in turmoil. The Roman Catholic party was very strong in the county, and staunch resistance was opposed by it to the new order of things ecclesiastical, a resistance which was, of course, well supported by the many wealthy religious houses which then abounded in the district. These latter, however, were suppressed by the King (Henry VIII.), and among them were the famous abbeys of Furness and Whalley, erstwhile seats of great monastic power. The Reformation then began to make great progress, especially in the south-eastern part of the county, and its development among the mercantile classes soon became particularly marked.

To quote the words of Halley : "The busy traders and manufacturers of Salfordshire, having formed mercantile connections with Holland and Germany, became acquainted with the great changes which had been so wonderfully wrought in the religion of those countries. Better educated than their rustic neighbours, and having more money to spare and more opportunity to spend it, they purchased books, conversed with foreigners, occasionally travelled to Continental fairs, knew more than their priests, prided themselves on a sturdy independence of thought, and became, many of them, firm and zealous adherents of the Reformation." It is at this period that we first begin to note the formation of a commercial class destined ultimately to become the most powerful factor in Lancashire life. Despite the tumult of political dissensions and the frequent conflicts of warring factions in the affairs of the State, the germ of business enterprise was beginning to expand into real and growing activity, and various branches of commerce and industry commenced to engage the energy and attention of a people eminently adapted by nature to carry all such undertakings to a prosperous issue. Fate had one more interruption to place in the path of Lancastrian progress in the seventeenth century, and this took the form of the great Civil War, which was very severely felt throughout the entire county. Particularly marked were the direful effects of this unhappy conflict at Manchester, Liverpool, Lancaster, Preston and Bolton, and many were the prodigies of valour performed on both sides, by Royalists and Parliamentarians alike. The supporters of the King displayed unexampled bravery and devotion in championing the royal cause, and among them none was more conspicuous for zeal and activity than the Earl of Derby, one of the great landed proprietors of Lancashire. We have all been thrilled by the story of the gallant defence of Latham House by that nobleman's courageous wife, the Countess of Derby, who, with the aid of a few gentlemen of the neighbourhood and a small garrison of retainers, defended this family seat for three whole months against the Parliamentary forces under Sir Thomas Fairfax. This heroic and successful achievement casts a lustre even upon such a deplorable and fratricidal struggle as the Civil War of that momentous period.

After the restoration of Charles II. peace came upon Lancashire, with all its attendant blessings; and the prosperity of the county began rapidly to increase. Trade and manufacture came promptly under the benign influence of political quietude and stability, and the commercial interests of the county were soon established upon a firm footing. Of course, this change for the better was not the work of a day. In most cases it was quite gradual, but in some instances the improvement was very rapid, and probably nowhere in England was the half-century immediately following the Civil War marked by more substantial progress in the useful arts than in Lancashire. With the exception of a brief commotion in the time of the Young Pretender and one or two outbreaks of popular irritation wholly connected with local industrial matters, the history of Lancashire during the last two centuries and a quarter has been uneventful in any other than a peaceful sense. To attempt to chronicle in these few pages the thousand and one achievements of science, practical skill, and commercial enterprise that have dis-

.tinguished this county during these two hundred years (or even during the century now approaching its close) would be a purely Quixotic undertaking. These great works of many and varied kinds speak for themselves in Lancashire's present greatness and influence. Through them she has become the foremost among English counties in return of revenues from all sources, and there is every reason to feel confident that what Lancashire men have accomplished in past and present times will be used by them and by their successors as stepping-stones to the still greater achievements of the years that are yet to come. With this we may drop the subject of Lancastrian history, and glance briefly at some of the natural causes that have influenced Lancastrian prosperity.

In the first place, the situation of the county is one of great advantage. Its position and its coast-line formation make it the natural outlet for the trade of north-western England, and its ports are the only ones accessible to large vessels between Milford Haven and the Clyde estuary. Lancashire lies between Westmoreland, Cumberland, Yorkshire, Cheshire, and the Irish Sea, and has an extreme length of eighty-five miles, and an extreme breadth of forty-six miles. The important district of Furness, where iron is abundant, is in the north, and is cut off from the main body of the county by Morecambe Bay and a part of Westmoreland. Between Yorkshire and Lancashire lie moors, mountains, and rivers. The interior is of a diversified character, hills and valleys alternating with level or undulating areas of considerable extent, and there are some fairly lofty eminences in the hilly districts, such as the "Conistan Old Man" and Pendle Hill, which are 2,640 and 1,850 feet above the sea-level respectively. The hills and mountainous tracts all subside towards the coast, which is remarkable for the absence of cliffs, and for the size of the bays by which it is indented. Morecambe Bay, and the estuaries of the Mersey, the Ribble, and the Wyre are the chief of these indentations.

Geologically considered, Lancashire is a very interesting county, and in its mineral wealth we have another important characteristic which is closely connected with the general prosperity of the whole district. In this respect coal holds the place of honour, and iron is closely associated with it, both being very largely produced in the county. The Lancastrian coalfield, considered in its entirety, is one of the largest in Great Britain, and has an estimated area of nearly 225 square miles, situated between the Rivers Mersey and Ribble, and comprising the several sub-sections of Burnley, Wigan, St. Helen's, Bolton, Manchester, &c. Very great enterprise and skill have been displayed in the development of the collieries in these several districts, and the magnitude of the coal-mining operations carried on in Lancashire may be gauged from the fact that, apart from the vast amount of coal worked for local consumption, there are upwards of 11,000,000 tons per annum taken out of the county, of which about 7,000,000 tons are shipped. During the last forty years the total output of the Lancashire collieries has more than doubled. In 1852 the amount raised was 8,225,000 tons. In 1880 the amount was no less than 19,120,000 tons, and in 1891 the total output was not far short of 23,000,000 tons, pretty evenly divided between the eastern and western coalfields of the county. The available coal supply of Lancashire has been recently estimated at over five billions of tons. The iron industry in this county presents a subject much too large for discussion here, but its importance is widely recognised and understood, and it has presented many opportunities for the advantageous display of Lancastrian enterprise.

We must not omit a word or two upon the agricultural aspect of Lancashire, despite the preponderance of commercial and manufacturing interests. The soil of the county presents many varieties of quality and character, but although one may meet with a great deal of barren and rocky moorland in the higher districts, there is much excellent land in the valleys of the numerous rivers, and in the vicinity of the seacoast. In these regions, where farming has received a due measure of careful attention, satisfactory results have ensued. Improved methods and the aids of science have certainly done much for agriculture in Lancashire in modern times, and, as a rule, all ordinary crops show to advantage. Oats are the principal corn crop, the climate being particularly suited for the growth of this grain. In the southern part of the county wheat is now a staple product of the farm, and in this fact we note a sign of advancement, for in former times only very small crops of wheat, barley, peas, &c., were grown. The potatoes of Lancashire have long maintained a high reputation, and in the neighbourhood of the large towns market-gardening is a profitable pursuit.

As a result of its proximity to the Atlantic Ocean, the climate of Lancashire is humid; and this has been said to beneficially affect the quality of the cotton yarns so largely spun in the county. The rainfall, however, is not so disagreeable as is the case in the districts along the East coast, where the influence of the Atlantic is not felt; and though Lancashire has the reputation of being a moist, not to say wet county, it is freer from heavy fogs than the greater part of maritime England.

The rivers of Lancashire, interesting as they undoubtedly are, can hardly be brought within the scope of the present article; but the chief stream, the Mersey, must always command special respect, if only for the manner in which it has been identified with the rise and growth of the mighty port of Liverpool. In this connection, however, it may be asserted with some truth that the Mersey shines with a reflected lustre, for in olden times its value as a waterway was not very great, and its present usefulness in commercial matters is chiefly due to the remarkable energy put forward by the people of Liverpool, Birkenhead, &c., in improving its not very promising resources, and in building up the wonderful system of unrivalled docks that now line its banks for miles, and provide accommodation for merchant ships from every land under the sun.

When we come to consider the splendid railway system of Lancashire, we are brought face to face with one of the greatest agents working for the welfare of this county. Nowhere in England are the facilities of railway transport from point to point more complete or more satisfactory than in Lancashire, and the men and the corporate bodies who have worked together in bringing this state of things to pass have performed a public service which cannot be too highly valued. There is, of course, an immense demand for easy and convenient means of rapid transit between the many busy towns of this tremendously busy region, and the supply, it must be confessed, is quite adequate to the requirement. There are five great lines of railway whose systems intersect this county, viz., the London and North-Western, the Lancashire and Yorkshire, the Furness, the Midland, and the Cheshire Lines; and at the present time a sixth line is in course of construction (the Lancashire, Derbyshire, and East Coast Railway), destined to afford through communication from the Mersey to the North Sea. The London and North-Western line issues from Cheshire at Runcorn, and runs to Newton, Wigan, Preston, Lancaster, and Kendal, sending out only a few branches along its lengthy route—one of these being from Warrington to Liverpool. This latter branch follows the course of the Mersey to Garston. At Ditton is the junction with the main-line branch from Prestonbrook *via* Runcorn, and the united traffic is taken from Garston to Liverpool by way of the important suburban station of Edge Hill. The St. Helen's branch of the London and North-Western Railway has a junction at Widnes with the Lancashire Union line. Another branch runs from Hest Bank to Morecambe; while the Longridge line and the line from Manchester to Leeds are also under the control of this Company.

The railways of Lancashire have taken the lead in England for many years past in efficient organisation and ample resource for dealing with the vast traffic they have to provide for. It must not be forgotten, too, that this county is to some extent the cradle of English railways, for the famous line opened in 1830 from Liverpool to Manchester (as a result of the North-Western Company's enterprise) was the first passenger line of any length in the kingdom, although the short line between Stockton and Darlington (opened for passengers in 1825) can claim a slight priority. For *local* traffic in Lancashire the Lancashire and Yorkshire line is pre-eminent. Its chief routes are as follows:—(1) From Liverpool to Ormskirk, Preston, Blackburn, Burnley, and Colne, with branches to Bootle and Southport, and to Wigan, Bolton, Bury, and Rochdale; (2) a cross line from opposite Runcorn, by St. Helen's and Rainford, to Ormskirk; (3) another cross line from Wigan to Southport; (4) Preston to Fleetwood (the Wyre Railway), with branches to Lytham and Blackpool; (5) Manchester to Bolton, Chorley, and Preston, with a branch to Wigan and Horwich; (6) Bolton to Blackburn, Whalley, and Clitheroe; (7) Manchester to Bury, Haslingden, and Accrington, with branch to Bacup and Rossendale. Manchester, Rochdale, Todmorden, and Burnley have connecting lines, from which branches go off to Middleton, Oldham, and Royton.

Between Partington and Cadishead the Cheshire Lines Railway enters the county, crossing the Mersey, and running into Liverpool *via* Warrington. At Grazebrooke Junction connections are effected with the Manchester and the Lancashire Union Railways, which lines traverse the coal-field and connect it with the Mersey ports. Entering the county near Hornby, and running down the Vale of Lune to Lancaster and Morecambe, the Midland Railway sends off numerous useful branches, and makes connection with the Furness Railway. A word or two of special mention must fall to the lot of the new line, the Lancashire, Derbyshire and East Coast Railway.

The project for this great undertaking—one of the largest railway enterprises promoted during recent years in England—was brought before Parliament in 1890, and received sanction in July of that year. About six months later arrangements were made with regard to the lettering of the first contract, comprising certain important works on the central section of the road, viz., between Chesterfield and Lincoln. A new Bill, introduced on behalf of the company, was passed in May, 1892, and the "first sod" was formally turned at Chesterfield on June 7th, 1892. This railway will provide a straight route across the country from east to west, starting at Warrington and running eastward to Sutton, a port on the coast of Lincolnshire. One very important section of the line is that which will traverse the coal districts of Derbyshire and Nottinghamshire, and there will be valuable connections with the systems of the Great Eastern and Great Northern Railway Companies. At the port of Sutton, the eastern terminus, suitable harbour and dock accommodation will be provided, and the line will thus become a very useful commercial factor. Its total length is about one hundred and thirty miles for the main line, and there will be upwards of forty miles of auxiliary lines. The capital of the company is stated at £7,500,000. Thus in railway enterprise, as in all other matters wherein capital and energy can be profitably employed, Lancashire still comes to the front, and shows an undiminished activity in promoting public convenience and commercial welfare. Here, again, the prominent men of the county play their part in various spheres of life, and the result of their labours is one of which they and their fellow-countrymen have every reason to be proud.

Lancashire is the birth-place of the English canal system for purposes of inland traffic. To be strictly accurate, one would have to admit that the first English canal was made in 1134 (*temp*. Henry I.), when the Trent was joined to the Witham. But the real inception of the canal system proper, by which our facilities of internal communication were so vastly improved in pre-railway days, can be traced to the Sankey Canal, the Act of Parliament authorizing the construction of which was obtained in 1755. This canal is ten miles long, and was constructed for the purpose of bringing coals from St. Helen's to Liverpool. It passes along the valley of the Sankey Brook, from which it takes its name, and enters the Mersey at Fidler's Ferry. Very soon after the inauguration of the Sankey Canal work was commenced on the Duke of Bridgewater's Canal, authorised by an Act of Parliament obtained in 1759. The canal was originally intended to afford a means of supplying Manchester with coal at a cheaper rate than by the Irwell and Mersey navigation, and was to connect the Duke of Bridgewater's collieries at Worsley with Manchester for this purpose. This being accomplished, the Duke obtained leave to extend his operations, and make a canal from the neighbourhood of Manchester into the Mersey. This he did, and soon afterwards the canal was extended from its former commencement at Worsley as far as the town of Leigh. In 1872 this important canal was purchased by the Bridgewater Navigation Company.

Another great Lancashire canal is the Leeds and Liverpool Canal, projected about 1770 by Mr. Longbottom of Halifax, and subsequently completed under the authority of several Acts of Parliament. It has a length of about 130 miles, and on its course passes by or near the busy towns of Burnley, Blackburn, Chorley, Wigan, and Burscough, eventually reaching Liverpool. The Lancaster Canal is about 70 miles long, and connects Preston, Lancaster, and Kendal. The Ashton Canal runs from Ashton-under-Lyne to Manchester, Stockport, Oldham, and Dukinfield, and connects these towns with the Huddersfield Canal. There are also in Lancashire the Rochdale Canal, the Ulverstone Canal, and the Bolton, Bury, and Manchester Canal. Despite the great increase of railway facilities, canals still remain in great favour for transport purposes, and it is estimated that there are 2,800 miles of canals in England alone—a fact which fully attests their importance, since in matters of this kind necessity, or at least expediency, is generally the prime motive.

Of course, it would be impossible to speak of the canals of Lancashire without making some allusion to that most gigantic and remarkable of all the canals of Britain, the Manchester Ship Canal; and at this point we may introduce a brief review of the inception and progress of what is not only a colossus among artificial waterways, but also one of the greatest engineering undertakings of the day. If there is one thing in which the energy and perseverance of the business men in Lancashire is triumphantly vindicated, it is the carrying out of just such enterprises as this—enterprises in which difficulties have to be encountered, obstacles overcome, and ultimate success achieved in the face of discouragement. The history of the Manchester Ship Canal is simply the story of perseverance victorious, told in a new way and upon a gigantic scale; and from this point of view the eventual prosperity of the undertaking must be a "consummation devoutly to be wished." That the Manchester Ship Canal will be commercially successful few people can doubt who have thoroughly studied its vast possibilities. In it, moreover, the Manchester people hail the realisation of a great dream and ambition, and its opening heralded the long-wished-for day when Manchester had free and uninterrupted communication with the sea, and now the ships of the world discharge their cargoes at the very doors of her busy warehouses. With such advantages as these in view it is not surprising that the people of the great "cotton metropolis" should have supported the Ship Canal with a resolute vigour that well deserves its anticipated reward. Apart from the manner in which Manchester's relations with the outer world will be altered and improved by this gigantic work, the whole of the commercial interests of the district promise to be greatly advanced thereby; and it is impossible not to view with satisfaction the approaching completion of a scheme which bids fair to result in great and substantial material benefits to a very large and important populative region.

It may not be out of place to briefly and succinctly trace the principal events in the history of the Ship Canal from the date of its inception to the present day. The project was taken up in downright earnest between eight and nine years ago, though it had doubtless been in embryo for some time; and in 1885 (July), the promoters of the scheme succeeded, after a well-contested struggle and a large expenditure of money, in obtaining the sanction of Parliament for the construction of the Ship Canal under certain conditions. This was the signal for great rejoicings in Manchester and throughout the whole district which was likely to reap most benefit from the canal, and many notable festivities marked the success of the first great movement in the work. When, however, the private preliminary prospectus of the Manchester Ship Canal Company was issued (October 8, 1885), the subscriptions received were not sufficient for requirements, owing to the fact that the Company had no power to pay interest out of capital during the construction of the Canal. This power was subsequently obtained by an Act of Parliament passed in June, 1886, and the subscription lists were opened July 20th, 1886, and closed on July 23rd. The full amount required was not, however, subscribed, and the issue was withdrawn. In the face of this disappointment a "Consultative Committee" was formed, comprising a number of influential gentlemen largely interested in the trade of the district. This committee, meeting under the auspices of Mr. Alderman Goldschmidt, then Mayor of Manchester, discussed the whole question of the Ship Canal earnestly and seriously, with a view to determining in the most exact manner possible the value of the various arguments for and against the scheme. As a result of these deliberations, the Consultative Committee arrived at the *unanimous* decision that, after leaving a margin amply sufficient for contingencies not foreseen, the Canal would, within two years of its opening, pay a dividend of not less than 5 per cent., besides showing a surplus equal to an additional 1 per cent. As a matter of fact, the volume of business which the Committee, after exhaustive enquiry felt justified in assuming would be done, was sufficient to warrant anticipations of a dividend of 8 per cent., or 3 per cent. more than that set down in their report. The effect of this report (which was signed by the Committee in November, 1886), was to greatly increase public confidence in the scheme of the Ship Canal, and in March, 1887, the Company issued a private circular in which they appealed to the inhabitants of Manchester to subscribe one-half of the required capital of £8,000,000. This amount of £4,000,000 was subscribed without delay, and in April, 1887, at a great public meeting in the Manchester Town Hall, a committee was formed to further influence subscriptions. On June 8, 1887, the Manchester Ship Canal Preference Shares Bill was read the first time in the House of Commons, and in due course passed through both Houses, receiving the Royal Assent on July 12, 1887. The Bill had for its object the division of the share capital of £8,000,000 into £4,000,000 of 5 per cent. perpetual preference shares, and £4,000,000 of ordinary shares, ranking for dividend after the preference shares, which latter were not to receive 5 per cent. until after the construction of the Canal, and both classes of shares receiving 4 per cent. alike until the Canal should commence operations. Immediately after the passing of this Bill subscription lists were opened for the £4,000,000 of perpetual 5 per cent. preference shares. On August 4, 1887, the Board of Trade duly certified that the Ship Canal Company complied with the conditions of its Act, whereby it was required to raise £5,000,000 of its share capital and an additional £1,710,000 as purchase-money of the Bridgewater Canal and the Mersey and Irwell Navigation, within two years of the passing of the Act.

We come now to the actual commencement of the work of construction, which was signalised on November 11, 1887, the formal ceremony of cutting the first sod of the Manchester Ship Canal Works being then performed at Eastham by Lord Egerton of Tatton, in the presence of the Board and some of the leading officials. From that time to this the work has gone steadily on, and now that it is completed, we are enabled to realise its magnitude and significance, and the great effects it is likely to produce. By this noble waterway the topography of one part of Lancashire has been completely changed, and Manchester has become to all intents and purposes a seaport. The achievement is a great one, not second even to that by which Ferdinand de Lesseps converted Africa into an island. Indeed, the Manchester Ship Canal is in several respects a greater and larger undertaking than the Suez Canal, this being especially true in regard to the labour involved and the nature of the difficulties contended with. What some of these difficulties were in the case of the Manchester enterprise may be understood by any one who surveys the country through which the canal passes. Apart from the stupendous work at Eastham, and the immensity of labour implied in some of the other cuttings and sections, there has all the while been the established overland and other traffic of the district to consider. These important points are illustrated in the various bridges that have been built to carry the public roads and railways across the canal, and in the remarkable arrangements that have been made for the Bridgewater Canal, which crosses the river Irwell at Barton. The idea of shutting up a portion of the water of a canal in an iron tank, and turning it out of its course in such a way as to admit of the passing-by of a ship in the great waterway beneath, is indeed worthy of the engineering genius of the period. The Bridgewater Canal, which the Ship Canal Company have purchased, and which they wish to preserve in its full usefulness, presented one of the greatest difficulties of the whole undertaking, and it has been dealt with in a manner most masterly and effective. It is very surprising to note the rapidity with which the work of constructing the Manchester Ship Canal has been performed. Despite all difficulties, only a little over six years were occupied in actual labour, and in that period wonders of engineering skill were accomplished. It is stated that about £15,000,000 has been expended on the Canal: certainly there is something to show, even for this vast outlay of money. The Canal has a length of 35 miles, and a depth throughout of 26 feet, with a minimum bottom width of 120 feet, which is increased to 170 feet for the $3\frac{1}{2}$ miles between Barton and Manchester. There are five sets of locks, viz., at Eastham, Latchford, Islam, Barton, and Manchester, and commodious docks at Manchester, Salford, and Warrington are also a part of the scheme. The Manchester docks have been completed, and offer ample accommodation for the shipping that will doubtless throng them before the world is a year older. The first lock of the Canal at Weston Marsh (designed to take the traffic between the River Weaver and the Ship Canal) was opened on April 16th, 1891. The first water was admitted into the Eastham section, where the main channel of the canal begins, on June 18th, 1891; and from Eastham to Saltport (about 10 miles) the Canal has been working regularly for some months. The passage of the first boats from Ellesmere Port down the Canal to the Mersey was made on July 12th, 1891.

The probable advantages of the Manchester Ship Canal seem to be very great indeed, and make us wonder that such an undertaking could ever have met with serious and continued opposition. In this respect, however, it has shared the lot of many another scheme that has ultimately conferred inestimable benefits upon mankind. The region influenced by the Manchester Ship Canal may be said to comprise something like 7,500 square miles, and to contain a population of at least 9,000,000. It is hard to conceive that anything but good can result from the bringing of such a district as this into closer commercial relationship with the great outer world. It is for the future to decide all this, and for our part we can see no reason to doubt the eventual prosperity of the whole undertaking. At all events, the Manchester Ship Canal will remain a striking tribute to the skill and resource of its talented engineer, Mr. E. Leader Williams, and a monument to the energy, zeal, and courage of those representative Lancashire men who have identified themselves with its history and championed its cause so faithfully and so effectually from first to last. The Manchester Ship Canal has, at least, the possibility of a splendid future. Everything just now points to the likelihood of its complete success; and our best wishes are for the full realisation of the many hopes that are centred in it to-day.

The roads of Lancashire, so greatly used by the traffic of the factory districts, both in former times and at the present day, are excellent. The principal coach roads are the following:—(1) The mail road between Port Patrick, Carlisle, and Manchester, entering the county at Stockport, and running by Manchester, Chorley, Preston, Garstang, and Lancaster, and thence passing away northwards through Westmoreland; (2) the Liverpool road, entering at Warrington, running by Prescot to Liverpool, and then on to Preston, where it joins the Carlisle road; (3) a road from Manchester through Oldham to Huddersfield and Leeds; (4) another northward to Bury, Haslingden, and Clitheroe, whence it runs into the Yorkshire mountain district. The coach road from Manchester joins the London and Liverpool road at Warrington. These are some of the principal highways of the county, but, of course, there are countless other roads and byways, and among them are several of those wonderful Roman roads which have withstood the wear and tear of centuries in such a remarkable manner. Five or six of these radiate from Manchester; one runs to Blackrod, one to Ribchester, two into Cheshire, one to Stockport, and one to Stretford. This latter is supposed by some archæologists to be that *Fines Flaviæ* to which reference is made by Richard of Cirencester.

Before closing this necessarily concise topographical survey of Lancashire, it may be well to glance at the county from the official point of view, and to note some of the important particulars set forth in the report of the last census. For political and statistical purposes there are two counties of Lancaster, the "Ancient" or "Geographical" county, and the "Administrative" county. The differences of boundary between these are too minute to be entered into here, but, as the greater contains the less, so does the "Ancient County" contain the "Administrative County." The former has four principal divisions, north, north-east, south-east, and south-west Lancashire, and these four are subdivided into twenty-three other divisions for parliamentary purposes. The county also includes the parliamentary boroughs of Barrow-in-Furness,

Blackburn, Bolton, Burnley, Bury, Liverpool, Manchester, Oldham, Preston, Rochdale, St. Helen's, Salford and Wigan, and parts of Ashton-under-Lyne, Stalybridge, Stockport, and Warrington. The city of Liverpool has nine divisions, that of Manchester has six, and the borough of Salford three.

In the "Ancient County" there are 730 entire ecclesiastical parishes or districts, and parts of ten others, and the whole is comprised in the dioceses of Carlisle, Chester, Liverpool, Manchester, Ripon, and Wakefield. The area of the "Ancient County" is 1,207,311 statute acres, and at the time of the census of 1891 it contained 765,230 inhabited houses, 59,277 uninhabited houses, 5,205 houses in course of building, and a population of 3,926,760, of which 1,889,926 were males, and 2,036,834 females.

The "Administrative County" includes eighteen municipal boroughs, has one Court of Quarter Sessions, and is divided into 34 Petty Sessional divisions. Twenty-five of the municipal and county boroughs have separate commissions of the peace, and the boroughs of Blackburn, Bolton, Oldham, Salford, Wigan, and the cities of Liverpool and Manchester have also separate Courts of Quarter Sessions. The area of the "Administrative County," with the county boroughs, is 1,202,726 statute acres, and in 1891 it contained 760,379 inhabited houses, 58,710 uninhabited houses, and 5,182 houses in course of building, the population being 3,906,721, divided into

1,880,715 males and 2,026,006 females. Such is some of the voluminous and interesting information supplied by the Census Report of 1891 concerning what may justly be termed England's "premier county," for, though it is sixth in actual area, Lancashire stands first among English counties in revenue from all sources, and, with the one exception of London, it has the largest population. The Lord Lieutenant of Lancashire is the Right Honourable the Earl of Sefton, K.G.

Of the trades and manufactures of Lancashire it is not possible to speak with any degree of fulness in the present article; but though any exhaustive comment upon the commercial aspect of the county is out of the question here, we cannot refrain from a few remarks upon those special departments of business life in which prominent Lancastrians have figured with so much distinction and success. Great, for example, is the fame that some have won in connection with the chief industry of the county, the altogether unequalled and unapproachable cotton trade of Lancashire. Here, alone, is a subject for volumes. In all the busiest districts of the county this trade is omnipresent. Vast amounts of capital are invested in it; thousands of hands find in it their means of livelihood; its mighty mills and factories dot the landscape far and near; and the ceaseless hum of the loom and the shuttle is heard on every side.

The rise and development of the cotton trade of

Lancashire must be regarded for all time as one of the most remarkable instances of the rapid growth of a great industry ever witnessed in this or any other country. Indeed, the whole history of cotton manufacture in Lancashire presents a series of surprises, and its advancement from the first has proceeded by leaps and bounds. Prior to the time of Charles I. we find no indication of cotton being imported into this country for purposes of clothing; but about 1641 it appears that fustian and velveteen were first made of cotton. About a hundred years later it is estimated that the entire manufacture of cotton in England did not produce more than £200,000 as the outcome of capital invested and labour performed. At that time the weavers were dispersed in cottages throughout what are now the manufacturing districts, and it was their custom to purchase their own materials, convert them into cloth, carry the fabric to market, and sell on their own account to the dealers. This, of course, could not possibly last, for the resources of supply would soon have been heavily overtaxed by the requirements of demand. The change began about the year 1760, when the Manchester merchants commenced to directly employ the weavers, furnishing them with materials, and paying for the labour of weaving. Then came the birth of the "factory system," caused by the invention of improved machinery of a character too complex to be worked in the cottages of the weavers. Hargreaves brought out his carding-engine in 1760, and seven years later his spinning-jenny multiplied many times over the products of the spinning-wheel, and effected as great a saving in labour as it produced an increase of output. By this time the trade was beginning to increase greatly in volume and importance, and its advancement was much accelerated when, in the year 1769, Arkwright brought out his spinning-frame, the advantage of which was that it enabled yarn to be made strong enough for warp. After a lapse of twenty years, or nearly that, Samuel Crompton attracted attention with his "spinning-mule," by which it was found possible to produce a much finer and softer quality of yarn than any previously turned out in this country. The importance of this at the time may be judged from the fact that Crompton sold some of his finest yarns at twenty guineas per pound. Yarns of similar fineness can be produced nowadays for a few shillings the pound. Since the days of Crompton, Arkwright, and Hargreaves the development in cotton machinery has been wonderful; indeed, in no branch of mechanical science has British inventive genius shone more brilliantly; and Lancashire, as the chief seat of the trade, can claim credit for the vast majority of these remarkable improvements. Dr. Cartwright's invention of the power-loom made weaving by power a possibility, and after that the growth of the trade began to be extraordinary. By the year 1787 the value of English cotton manufactures rose to nearly

£7,000,000. In 1832 it was estimated at £25,000,000. In 1841 Mr. Porter's estimate placed it at £49,000,000. At the present day the value may be placed at upwards of £100,000,000. In Lancashire there are nearly 1,800 spinning-mills and cotton factories in operation, representing over 42,000,000 spindles and 610,000 looms, and giving employment to something like 250,000 hands. The capital invested in the cotton industry is estimated at upwards of £100,000,000. There can be no doubt that the stimulus of the cotton trade has been felt throughout the whole of industrial Lancashire, with highly beneficial results. Many other trades, bearing relationship in some degree or manner to this staple industry, have sprung up and flourished greatly in the county. The making of machinery and apparatus for cotton-spinners and manufacturers is doubtless the chief of these kindred industries, and it has been brought to a remarkable state of perfection by the enterprise and progressive zeal of the numerous firms that have engaged in it. The largest manufacturers of cotton machinery in the world are found in Lancashire, and their productions are universally famous.

The engineering industries of the county have also been developed upon a very large scale, while shipbuilding, iron and steel manufacture, glass manufacture, the making of watches and clocks, and the productions of hats, pottery, soap, chemicals, leather, wire, brass goods, &c., &c., rank prominently among the many other manufacturing enterprises in which Lancashire capital, energy, and labour are employed. Manchester is the world's cotton mart, and "Manchester goods" are famous the wide world over. Whole nations are supplied with the multifarious manufactures of cotton, silk, and wool that are gathered together in the warehouses of this busy city; and these various fabrics represent the many diverse products of this county's enormous textile industry, in the different branches of which the output of novelties is maintained from year to year with untiring energy and apparently inexhaustible resource. Of the vast trade of Liverpool, and the many great commercial interests centred in that city, it is unnecessary to speak in detail here. The high standing of this port is universally recognised, and the importance of the part it has played for many years in maintaining effective communication between the manufacturing centres of Lancashire and the markets of the outer world needs no indication.

Having now in some measure reviewed the natural resources of the county of Lancashire, and glanced at some of the principal spheres of activity in which those resources are turned to practical account, it is time to direct our attention to the men whose lives and works have in many cases left a deep and lasting impression upon the condition of the county, and have helped to place it in its present position of distinction, not merely as a prosperous seat of trade, but also as a region in which municipal, social, educational, and artistic progress are all studied with care and promoted with judgment and liberality. Few counties have given birth to so many men of mark in the different walks of life in which national celebrity may be attained; and a biography of notable Lancastrians, past and present, would contain a remarkably large number of names familiar to the general ear from their association with achievements of special import. From this long list it is difficult to make a selection for particular mention here, but among the many who now rest from their labours, and whose works live after them, there are some whose names it would be impossible to omit from any work dealing biographically with Lancashire.

Who, for instance, could think of the county's staple industry without remembering Richard Arkwright, James Hargreaves, and Samuel Crompton?—the first the inventor of the spinning-frame, the second the inventor of the spinning-"jenny," and the third the inventor of the "mule." These three men have been justly said to have originated the cotton-spinning trade as it is carried on to-day, and with them must be associated Dr. Cartwright, whose power-loom revolutionised the methods of the cotton factories, and was the prototype of the wonderfully ingenious weaving machinery now in use in all the great cotton-works of Lancashire. Other names appear in connection with the same trade, though less prominently, such as those of John Kay, of Bury, who invented the fly-shuttle; Robert Kay, the originator of the drop-box; Horrocks, the improver of the power-loom; and William Lee, who invented the stocking-frame as far back as the year 1589. Of the three or four great inventors identified with the early history of cotton manufacture in Lancashire, both James Hargreaves and Crompton died comparatively poor. Arkwright seems to have profited by his invention. He amassed a great fortune, and received the honour of knighthood.

In quite another sphere of industrial activity we find the name of Henry Cort. He was born in 1740, and to him is due the practical application and complete development of the process of converting pig-iron into bar or malleable iron. He also introduced the process of puddling. Among British travellers the name of Captain James King is familiar. He was a Lancashire man, and was the companion of Captain Cook on his last voyage. George Romney, the artist, is another Lancastrian whose reputation is national. Born in 1734, he attained to great eminence in pictorial art, and Flaxman pronounced him "the greatest of all British painters in poetic dignity of conception."

John Dalton, the originator of the atomic theory, was a native of Lancashire; and so was William

Roscoe, whose name will ever be venerated in Liverpool, and whose voluminous writings are a monument to his self-acquired learning as well as to his intellectual powers. Another famous Lancastrian was Dr. Whewell, the author of the "History of the Inductive Sciences," and of whose name it was jocularly said that it was easier to whistle it than to pronounce it.

And so the list runs on, revealing, as we glance down it, many another name known to fame, not the least noteworthy being those that have gained distinction in literature and intellectual pursuits. Thomas de Quincey, the author of that fascinating work, "The Confessions of an Opium-Eater," was of this latter number. So was Mrs. Hemans, the poetess; Bamford, the weaver poet; and Mrs. Gaskell, whose novels display such a remarkable power of observation and such marked talent for the delineation of character. Richard Cobden, the great advocate of free trade, though born in Sussex, became associated at an early age with the Manchester cotton trade, and he occupied for a long time a house at the lower end of Quay Street, Manchester, which became the first habitation of the now extensive and famous Owens' College.

Mention of this important academical institution reminds us of the educational advantages conferred upon Lancashire by the beneficence of certain Lancashire men. All over the county instances may be met with, and in Manchester and Liverpool they are particularly numerous. The Owens' College is especially noteworthy in the former city, and originated in consequence of the bequest of Mr. John Owens, a Manchester merchant, who, dying in 1846, left the residue of his property after paying legacies and charitable bequests, to trustees for educational purposes. The college was formerly opened in March, 1851, occupying the house till then tenanted by Richard Cobden. At the present day the college is suitably accommodated in a handsome and spacious edifice which is one of the architectural ornaments of the city. The late Sir James Whitworth, Bart., whose fame in the engineering and mechanical world is international, was a large benefactor to Owens' College; and the late Mrs. Abel Heywood left £10,000 free of legacy duty to form an endowment, "the income arising from such endowment to be applied for the purposes of making proper provisions for the instruction of women in the said college, in such manner as the governors of the said college shall think fit."

Another Lancashire worthy was the benevolent founder of Chetham's hospital and library at Manchester, which institution has one of the oldest and most interesting free libraries in England; and yet another of the same liberal-minded and far-seeing type was Hugh Oldham, who, as long ago as 1515, founded the Manchester Grammar School, so justly esteemed for its excellent record and high standing in the scholastic world. It must not be forgotten that Lancashire can claim the honour of being the birthplace of one of the most distinguished politicians and men of letters of the century, the Right Hon. W. E. Gladstone, who was born in Liverpool on December 29th, 1809; and in the pages which here follow we shall have opportunity of mentioning the names of many other living Lancashire men who are maintaining the traditions of the county in enterprise, intellectual advancement and public spirit.

Chapter II.

MANCHESTER.

THE INDUSTRIAL METROPOLIS OF THE WORLD.

GENERALLY speaking, it may be remarked of cities, as it has been of men, that "some are born great, some achieve greatness, and some have greatness thrust upon them." Numerous instances in point might be cited from ancient and modern history in all parts of the world, but our own country, especially in recent times, has been peculiarly productive of towns and cities pertaining to the second of these three classes—communities of men that have achieved greatness by the sheer force of their innate energies and resources. Manchester has very strong claims to be regarded as one of the brightest examples of what may be accomplished in this direction. The powers of enterprise and progress so strikingly manifested at all times by the people of Lancashire present an epitome of their results in the great civic individuality of Manchester, where some of the county's mightiest industrial forces are focussed, and where the trade created by those forces finds a centre from which its ramifications may be extended to every quarter of the globe. This process of commercial expansion has recently been enormously facilitated by an achievement of which not Manchester alone, but the whole nation, is justly proud. Time was when Manchester realised every ideal of a purely industrial city, using the word "industrial" as making a distinction from "commercial." Its huge factories, its smoke-laden atmosphere, its turbid river, its army of toiling artisans, all proclaimed the extent to which the city and its people were involved in labours of production. These conditions still obtain, but they have been amplified, and the domain of Manchester's activity has been enlarged. The factories are still there, the "incense of industry" still floats in clouds above the tops of countless towering chimneys, the throngs of busy workers are more numerous than ever, and the whirr of gearing and the hum of machinery resounds in a hundred streets, whence emanate a thousand different wares for the use and benefit of the peoples of the earth. But there is now something more than all this. A new element has come into the city's life, and though we are many miles from the "sounding sea," we meet in the street bronzed and weather-beaten sailors, we hear people talk of docks and shipping, and anon we find ourselves face to face with the great fact that Manchester is no longer dependent upon the "iron

THE MANCHESTER TOWN HALL.

horse" for her communication with the ocean. Of all the greatness she has achieved in the long course of her history there is none greater than this—that she has made herself a pathway to the sea, and established for herself a direct intercourse with the markets of other lands by which the whole of her vast commerce, present and prospective, is placed entirely under her own control.

Independence, then, as typified by the Ship Canal, is the keynote of the new era in Manchester, the watchword of that larger life in which she will figure not alone as a producer but also as a universal distributor—no longer looking to the good offices of intermediary ports in her dealings with the great world beyond the seas, but conducting her business *in propriâ personâ* with every market in which there is demand for her productions. Manchester, as a seaport, places an entirely new face upon the trade of a very large area of Lancashire, and the facilities she now affords for the cheaper transport of cotton (to say nothing of many other materials hardly less important) will extend the benefits of her enterprise to many other manufacturing centres that have already derived a large measure of advantage from the market conveniences she has always provided. Indeed, there is hardly any limit to the possibilities foreshadowed by the auspicious completion and inauguration of the Manchester Ship Canal. It opens up a new outlet for many inland industries, and a new inlet for many foreign products; and, properly worked, as it is sure to be, it should prove a factor of the very highest potency in promoting the expansion of every branch of commercial activity in northern and north-western England. We have dealt especially upon this great waterway and its capabilities for the reason that it has become the dominant agent of progress in Manchester, and one of the busiest districts of the Kingdom, and also because it is a magnificent testimony to the spirited energy and mercantile instincts of the Lancastrian people. Her Majesty the Queen, when she graciously honoured this gigantic achievement by her presence at the inaugural ceremony, was pleased to say that she recognised in the Ship Canal a "further evidence of the unceasing energy and enterprise of her subjects"; and all who have acquainted themselves with the nature of the work, and with the importance of the issues dependent upon it, must surely feel a sincere admiration for the courage that could conceive and support so tremendous an undertaking, and for the skill and perseverance that have carried it to a happy completion. Lancashire in general, and Manchester in particular, teem with evidences of the power of hard work and fixity of purpose; and the Manchester Ship Canal, the glory of the city and the county alike, bear witness to the fact that these two attributes are as actively existent in the Lancashiremen of to-day as they were in their staunch and thrifty forefathers.

There is no necessity to go farther than the Ship Canal for proofs of what Manchester men are able to accomplish. It is recorded that when the Ship Canal was on the point of completion, a resident in this city, commenting upon the approaching triumph of his fellow-citizens' enterprise, said: "What Manchester means, Manchester will do." This seems to us to sum up the whole character of the Lancashire Industrial Metropolis in six words, and there we may well be content to leave the matter, knowing from past experience that what Manchester "means" will be for the good of the nation, as far as the intelligent promotion of commerce and the useful arts can contribute thereto.

Some account has already been given in these pages of the inception of the Manchester Ship Canal, and of the circumstances under which the work of construction was undertaken and proceeded with. Now that the six years of labour (from the cutting of the first sod in November, 1887, to the completion of the entire work at the close of 1893) have borne their full fruit, it will not be out of place to here record the successful accomplishment of this gigantic piece of engineering, and the realisation of many of the hopes and expectations centred in the project of connecting Manchester with the sea. The actual completion of the Ship Canal may be said to coincide with the date of the opening of the great waterway for traffic on Monday, January 1st, 1894. On that day, amid much enthusiasm on the part of the people of Manchester, and of the region through which the Canal takes its course, the Directors of the Ship Canal Company, with the Corporations of Manchester and Salford, and several other public bodies, made a sort of triumphal progress from Latchford Locks to Manchester, a distance of about twelve miles; and the presence of many thousands of spectators from far and near lining the banks all along the route, testified to the intensity of the popular interest taken in this proceeding. As the event was, in some measure, an historical one, it may be well to note particularly a few of its details. The procession through the Canal was headed by the *Norseman*, the fine yacht of Mr. S. R. Platt, a member of the board, bearing the Directors of the Company. Following came the *Snowdrop*, with the members of the Manchester Corporation, and in her wake the large steamer *Crocus* conveyed many of the relations and friends of that great civic body, which had so liberally and courageously come to the assistance of the Ship Canal in time of need. The *Great Britain* was next in order, having the Salford Corporation on board; and after this came other boats bearing the Warrington Town Council, the members of the Manchester Conservative Club, the Manchester Arts Club, and other institutions. A press correspondent describes the scene as a pretty and imposing one, the vessels steaming along, gaily decked with bunting of many bright colours. Altogether about twenty vessels joined in the procession and as the day was gloriously fine there was nothing to detract from the complete success of this interesting and official function. Deafening cheers from multitudes of people on the quays and docks at Pomona and Salford greeted the arrival of the leading steamers, and well might they cheer, for on that day Manchester became a seaport for all practical purposes, and the aspirations of years were fulfilled. Noteworthy was the fact that vessels bearing all kinds of merchandise followed in the train of the official procession, the stream of traffic being kept up until a late hour in the evening; and the future maritime relations of Manchester and Salford with the great outer world were foreshadowed in the arrival of the *Lamprey* from Glasgow, with a general cargo; of the *Bittern* from Antwerp; and of several vessels from London and the Continent generally. Everybody knows that prodigies of labour and marvels of engineering skill attended the construction of this, our greatest canal; but the actual "facts and figures" which so strikingly illustrate the stupendous character may not be quite so generally familiar. Here are a few. While the work of construction was in progress there were sometimes as many as sixteen thousand men employed, the average number engaged throughout being about ten thousand. But if the entire labour of excavation had been dependent upon the efforts of these workers with pick and shovel, most of us would have been "very old ghosts" indeed (as Dr. Wendell Holmes once said) ere the Manchester Ship Canal became an accomplished fact. The marvel of marvels in this huge undertaking was the work performed by the "steam navvies" and "excavators," of which ponderous engines no fewer than one hundred were in operation along the route. Each of these mighty machines (it is said on the authority of Lord Egerton of Tatton) was capable of doing the work of two thousand men. Obviously, therefore, the labour of two hundred thousand men was represented in this way alone. Only a limited number of horses were at work at any time upon the Canal, but an enormous horse-power was represented in the 176 locomotives, 194 steam cranes, 209 steam pumps, and 200 other steam engines almost constantly kept at work for various purposes; and from first to last something like 725,000 tons of coal were consumed in feeding the furnaces of these different types of motors and mechanical agents. It is estimated that the total quantity of earth and rock displaced by the excavation was over fifty million cubic yards, or about seventy million tons; and statisticians have computed that this vast bulk of material would form some sixteen monuments of the size of the Great Pyramid, and would load a hundred and fifty millions of wheelbarrows, which, placed end to end, would encircle the earth about eight times. From the fact that seventy millions of bricks were used in the brickwork of the Canal, it has been "figured" that these would build houses for three thousand families, or make a wall six feet high for a distance of 452 miles. What *should* we do without statisticians? Their labours may be "dry," but how forcibly they illustrate truths that might otherwise remain incomprehensible.

A rapid run through the Manchester Ship Canal, from Eastham to the terminus at "Cottonopolis," may serve to further indicate the importance of this remarkable work. The once quiet little village of Eastham, with its ancient church and its pleasure gardens, beloved of Liverpudlian excursionists, has been vigorously roused from its lethargy by the advent of Manchester's highway to the sea. It owes this awakening to its position, which was found to be suitable for the first locks on the great Canal. Entering here from the broad Mersey, we find that three massive locks have been constructed, respectively 600 feet by 80 feet, 350 feet by 50 feet, and 150 feet by 30 feet, besides two sluices, to help the filling of the Canal. These three entrances to the Canal are so contrived that vessels can be admitted at almost any state of the tide. The wonderful hydraulic machinery, supplied by Messrs. Armstrong, enables the ponderous lock-gates to be swung open with the utmost ease. Passing on, we come to Ellesmere Port, three miles up from Eastham, where the Shropshire Union Railway has its terminus, and the Canal

LOCKS AND ENTRANCE TO THE MANCHESTER SHIP CANAL AT EASTHAM.

connects with the London and North-Western system. Here there is ample wharfage, a pontoon, and a ship-repairing yard; and here, too, we note the first tidal opening to the sand flats of the Mersey, with a remarkable weir-like structure, of vast extent, in which thousands of timber piles have been driven. Another engineering feat is the carrying of the little river Gowie under the Canal by means of syphons—one of the many instances in which the constructors of the great waterway have triumphed over natural obstacles without appreciably disturbing the existing order of things. For the next six miles or so the Mersey skirts the Canal, with only a narrow strip of land between, and then we come to a " new town," something rarely seen in this old-established land of ours. This is Saltport, appropriately named, for it is the outlet of the Cheshire salt trade. Saltport is built upon the marshes at the junction of the Ship Canal with the River Weaver, and here also are the Weston and the Runcorn and Weston Canals. A side-lock at Weston Marsh enables vessels of considerable size to proceed up to Nantwich. There are excellent wharves and jetties at Saltport, and many ships of large tonnage discharged cargoes here before the Canal was completed at Manchester. Within the next few miles, communication is effected with the Shropshire Canal and the Bridgewater Canal, which means, among other important commercial advantages, that the Staffordshire potteries now have a

THE MANCHESTER SHIP CANAL: UNDER THE RUNCORN VIADUCT.

direct sea and canal route for the reception of Cornish stone and clay, the two principal materials of the ceramic industries of Stoke, Hanley, Longton, etc. The noble viaduct of the London and North-Western Railway at Runcorn is one of the "sights" *en route*, and a little higher up, the Mersey begins to turn off towards Warrington, having apparently "had enough" of the society of its great rival. We next notice the first of the several swing-bridges, by which certain high roads are carried across the Canal. These huge and weighty structures work with astonishing ease—another proof of the efficacy of Messrs. Armstrong's hydraulic machinery. The last of the Mersey tidal openings is soon passed, and we go on towards Latchford. At the Vyrnwy Subway the Liverpool water supply is carried elliptically under the Canal. At Moore Lane we pass the second swing bridge, and three others come in succession, as well as the High Level Cantilever Bridge and several viaducts, before we come to Latchford Locks. These are the first locks above Eastham, from which they are 21 miles distant. Their measurements are 600 feet by 65 feet, and 350 feet by 45 feet, the rise being $16\frac{1}{2}$ feet. On past Warburton and the viaduct of the Cheshire Lines, from Warrington to Stockport, and our next point of note is Partington, where the arrangements for coal shipping are upon a very complete scale. The basin has an area of about five acres, and there are most extensive quays, with every

BARTON SWING AQUEDUCT, CARRYING THE OLD BRIDGEWATER CANAL ACROSS THE SHIP CANAL.

facility for loading. Presently we reach another viaduct of the Cheshire Lines (Manchester and Liverpool route); and then in succession come Irlam Locks, 28 miles from Eastham and 7 miles from Manchester, with a rise of 16 feet; and Barton Locks, two miles nearer Manchester, with a rise of 15 feet. At Irlam, the Mersey and the Irwell meet. At Barton the most remarkable contrivance on the whole Canal comes before our notice, for here, by means of the Barton Aqueduct, the Bridgewater Canal is carried bodily over the Ship Canal, without disturbing the operation of the latter, and with only a momentary interruption of the course of the former. The plan adopted is as bold as it is successful. When it becomes necessary for a vessel to pass in the Ship Canal, the pendent portion of the Bridgewater Canal is simply shut up in a colossal sort of tank, and is then swung easily upon a pivot until its transverse position is changed into a parallel one. Then it is swung back again, and traffic proceeds on the Bridgewater Canal until the manœuvre has to be repeated. Nothing could speak more plainly for the resolution of the Ship Canal authorities to carry their great work through in the face of all difficulties, or for the ingenuity they have displayed in the attainment of their object.

The "beginning of the end" is reached at Mode Wheel Locks, $33\frac{1}{2}$ miles from Eastham, for at this point the extensive system of docks for Salford and

BARTON SWING AQUEDUCT, AS SEEN FROM THE CANAL.

Manchester practically commences. The Salford Docks have no less than 71 acres of water and 129 acres of quay space, the length of quays amounting to 3¾ miles. Here, indeed, is a "harbour" calculated to astonish the visitor; but this is not all, for we have yet to reach the docks of Manchester itself, where there are 33 acres of water and 23 acres of quay space, the length of quays being 1¾ miles. Both at Salford and Manchester Docks there are several navigable arms, and Ordsall Dock occupies a considerable space by itself. The plan of the entire docks is excellent, having been carefully thought out with a view to affording the utmost possible convenience to each class of trade. All these arrangements are now beginning to justify themselves, and already the "argosies of commerce," which once stayed their course at Liverpool, have become a familiar spectacle to the people of the "cotton capital." The completion of the Ship Canal is certainly a high honour to the City of Manchester and the Borough of Salford, and we venture to think that most people will agree with us in saying that by the energy and determination with which this gigantic enterprise has been carried out honour has been done and renown added to the entire nation. The individual names associated with the great work are now too well known to need recapitulation. Some of the most prominent men of Manchester and Salford have actively interested themselves in the

THE DOCK AT MANCHESTER.

project from the first, and have done their part to secure its furtherance at every stage of its by no means uneventful history. Surely nothing less than Lancastrian perseverance and Lancastrian "pluck" could have achieved such a triumph over tremendous obstacles as this thirty-five miles of waterway undoubtedly is. Lord Egerton of Tatton, the Chairman of the Board of Directors, has taken a deep and active interest in the whole undertaking, loyally supported by his colleagues, and by many local men whom to name would be superfluous; and Mr. E. Leader Williams, the talented engineer of the Canal, has assuredly left us no room or reason for comment upon his share of the work, since the Canal itself and its thousand and one interesting details form a noble monument to his genius and ability.

As to what the Canal will accomplish for Manchester and a large part of Lancashire now that it is actually in working order—that is a matter which it would be idle to discuss here. Time will show us this, as well as many other things, and it is enough for the present to say that the expressed opinions of many experienced and far-seeing business men in all departments of commercial enterprise encourage lively hopes of ultimate success. Indeed, the Canal can hardly fail to bring anything but large benefit to the industries and trades of this district, if only on account of the marked saving it effects in the cost of transporting goods, as compared with the old system.

THE ACTON GRANGE VIADUCT OVER THE MANCHESTER SHIP CANAL.

Thus cotton now comes at 7s. per ton freight, instead of 13s. 8d. as formerly *viâ* Liverpool, and there are similarly striking reductions in connection with all other important commodities. Manifest advantages will accrue to many notable industrial concerns not only along the route of the Canal and in the vicinity of Manchester, but also at more distant points, which now have a new and improved means of communication with the ocean; and not the least noteworthy item in the varied train of results that must undoubtedly follow the opening of the Ship Canal is the great increase to be looked for in the population of Manchester itself, where many new commercial and manufacturing interests are certain to develop themselves, side by side with those already existing. It will perhaps be interesting to state that the first cargo of cotton to come direct to Manchester by steamer, arrived on January 15th, 1894, by the steamer *Finsbury* (1,909 tons register), which brought 4,170 bales, or 1,000 tons of cotton. The first cargo of cattle brought *viâ* the Ship Canal arrived from Belfast on January 8th, 1894, the incident causing a great amount of interest.

It now only remains to chronicle the crowning event in the early history of the Manchester Ship Canal—an event long to be remembered with gratification by all concerned in the enterprise itself, as well as by the people of Lancashire in general. We refer, of course, to the formal opening of the great waterway on May 21st, 1894, when Her Majesty the Queen was graciously pleased to honour this achievement of her loyal northern subjects by performing the inaugural ceremony in person. Twice before the Queen had visited Manchester, and on this her third journey to the busy Lancastrian metropolis, she must have noticed many evidences of the progress that has been made in the city since Her Majesty's second visit in 1857. On the arrival of the royal train at London Road Station, the Lord Mayor of Manchester (now Sir Anthony Marshall), with the Town Clerk, the Reception Committee, the Lord Lieutenant, the High Sheriff, and the General Officer in Command, received Her Majesty on the platform, and the Lord Mayor was presented to the Queen by Earl Spencer, the Minister in attendance. In the streets a most enthusiastic reception was accorded to the Sovereign by the vast multitudes assembled from all parts of the country, and, it may truly be said, from nearly every quarter of the kingdom. Her Majesty received loyal addresses of welcome from the Corporation and from Owens' College, to which she returned gracious replies.

Proceeding then to the scene of the day's function at Trafford Wharf, the Queen was received in the Royal Pavilion by Lord Egerton of Tatton (Chairman of the Ship Canal Company), and by the other Directors and principal officers, the Chairman being presented in due form by Earl Spencer. Her Majesty then went on board the Admiralty yacht *Enchantress*, in which she was to go to Mode Wheel for the performance of the opening ceremony. The Chairman of the Company, Lord Egerton, thereupon presented the following address : " The work which your Majesty is graciously pleased to inaugurate is one of supreme importance not only to the great commercial and manufacturing district of which Manchester is the centre, but to the nation, providing as it does direct communication with all parts of the world. The Manchester Ship Canal follows as nearly as possible the ancient river boundary between your Majesty's Duchy of Lancaster and the County of Chester for a distance of $35\frac{1}{2}$ miles ; its construction has occupied a period of seven years, and it may claim to rank as one of the greatest engineering achievements of your Majesty's beneficent and prosperous reign. We rejoice to think that your Majesty's reign has been coincident with the greatest extension of scientific knowledge, expansion of commerce, and development of the peaceful arts of which the world holds record ; and we believe that this great work will bring into closer commercial union the whole of your Majesty's vast empire. We earnestly trust that the future of this important enterprise may prove to be worthy of the high distinction which your Majesty's gracious presence has conferred upon it, and that it may further promote the prosperity of your Majesty's loyal subjects at home and abroad."

The following reply was returned on behalf of the Queen : "It is with great pleasure that I receive your address and am able to be present at the opening of the Manchester Ship Canal. I recognise in this great and most important undertaking, and the admirable engineering skill with which it has been constructed, further evidence of the unceasing energy and enterprise of my subjects. I trust that the increased facilities to be afforded by it for direct commercial intercourse by sea with the trade of the world will not fail to be of the greatest advantage to the busy and industrial population of Manchester and the neighbouring district, and I earnestly pray that, by God's blessing, this work may contribute to the well-being and happiness of all classes of my subjects in the United Kingdom."

The Directors having been presented to Her Majesty by Lord Egerton, Lord Carrington (the Lord Chamberlain) summoned into the Royal presence the Lord Mayor of Manchester (Mr. Anthony Marshall), and the Queen conferred upon him the honour of Knighthood, a similar honour being subsequently bestowed upon Mr. Alderman Bailey, the Mayor of Salford. The Queen then proceeded in the *Enchantress* to Mode Wheel, and, pressing a button by which the hydraulic machinery opening the lock gates was set in motion, said: "I have now great pleasure in declaring the Manchester Ship Canal open," whereupon a rocket signal was discharged, a salute of twenty-one guns was fired, and the ringing cheers of the spectators proclaimed the accomplishment of the gracious act by which the Sovereign of England bestowed her Royal sanction upon an enterprise worthy of the great nation over which she rules. Thus, with all the pomp and ceremonial of regal and civic dignity, was inaugurated that mission of usefulness which the Manchester Ship Canal is designed to fulfil. Its destinies are in good keeping, and it may be confidently expected that the energy and ability, the tenacity of purpose and businesslike vigour, which have brought this remarkable waterway into actual existence, will be so combined in the further administration of its affairs as to secure to the people of Lancashire and the kingdom generally the fullest measure of benefit obtainable from its operation.

As to the city itself, every black spot and unsavoury region within the municipal boundaries is being rapidly purified and beautified. No people in England are more ready to display a really generous liberality in all matters concerning the condition of their town than those of Manchester, and this is amply proven by the internal aspect of the city, with its well-kept streets and its stately public buildings and commercial edifices. Manchester, at the same time, is a city of paradoxes. It is at once the newest and the oldest of English towns; it is the centre of a vast manufacturing district, and yet is not itself, strictly speaking, a manufacturing town; it is one of the plainest, and at the same time one of the handsomest, cities in the kingdom; it unites within itself the acme of wealth and the depth of poverty; it is a cathedral city, yet a stronghold of Nonconformity; it has an enormous Roman Catholic population, but is one of the most Protestant communities in England; and, finally, it has in proportion to its population probably more teetotallers than any other British town, and yet a vast quantity of strong liquor is consumed within its limits. The wonders of Manchester are inexhaustible, and the city stands as a mighty monument to the vigour and energy of its people.

In his preface to "The Manchester Rebels of the Fatal '45," the late Mr. W. Harrison Ainsworth wrote:—"Little of the old town is now left. The lover of antiquity—if any such should visit Manchester—will search in vain for those black-and-white timber habitations, with pointed gables and latticed windows, that were common enough seventy years ago. Entire streets embellished by such houses have been swept away by the course of modern improvements, but I recollect them well." At the same time within the city of Manchester the number of factories is yearly decreasing. There is still a forest of chimneys, and the atmosphere contains a full allowance of smoke, but the fuliginous pall which overhangs the place is an indispensable accompaniment of every great and populous city, and does not now signify, as it once did, the existence of a host of manufactories in the very heart of the town itself. The Corporation of Manchester (whose administration of local affairs is deserving of the highest commendation) have expended very large sums of money in beautifying and improving the city, while private enterprise and the public spirit of the inhabitants have done almost, if not quite, as much in the same direction. The change thus wrought within the last thirty years has been something magical. In the "sixties" the well-known Deansgate was little more than a narrow, dirty lane, not at all prepossessing, imposing, or attractive. To-day Deansgate is one of the handsomest thoroughfares in England. The old Town Hall has been replaced by a structure which is hardly surpassed in beauty and majesty among the municipal buildings of Europe. Manchester also boasts Assize Courts and Police Courts such as are to be found nowhere else in the country; and the new Royal Exchange ranks with the grandest and most imposing edifices of its kind in England.

Manchester and Salford are, as we have said, usually spoken of as one town, and this is justified by the fact that they are connected by ties of the most intimate kind. Each has its Mayor and Corporation, its separate local administration, its own local rating, and its own way of managing its affairs; yet the leading men in the two places are identical. The manufacturer who has his mills or his works of any kind in Salford has his offices in Manchester, and

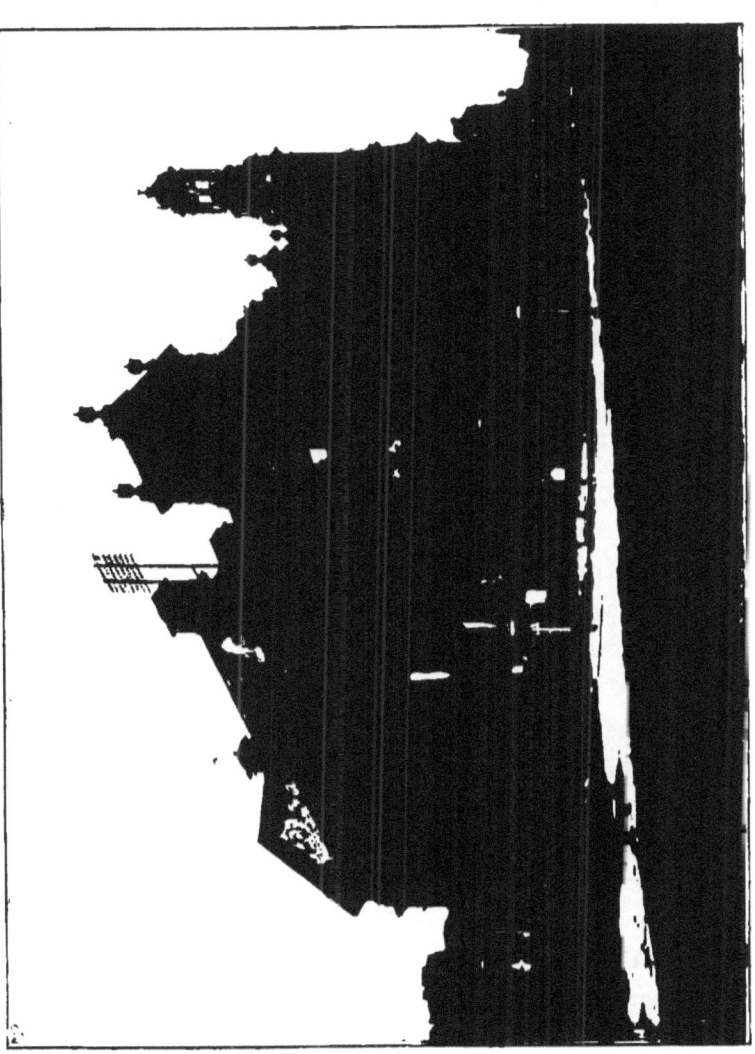

F. Frith & Co.] THE ROYAL EXCHANGE. [Reigate.

transacts his business on the Manchester Exchange. Salford is, in fact, mainly the working-class suburb of "Cottonopolis," and fulfils towards it much the same function as that of Southwark to London. It is also the seat of a Roman Catholic bishopric. Between the two towns flows the turbid stream of the river Irwell, once a very beautiful river, but now anything but attractive owing to the prosaic and matter-of-fact nature of its surroundings. On the high ground above the Irwell stands the cathedral of Manchester, the "Old Church," as it is still familiarly termed. The foundation of this fane is a very ancient one, and it was made a collegiate church as far back as 1422. Soon after 1830 the old collegiate foundation, governed by a warden, was abolished, and the Deanery was established, the first occupant of the decanal stall under this new constitution being the Hon. and Very Rev. W. Herbert. In 1847 the bishopric was created, and the first bishop of Manchester was Dr. Prince-Lee. His successor, the late Dr. Fraser, was a man of high scholarly attainments, and was greatly beloved in the diocese. The present bishop is the Right Rev. James Moorhouse, D.D., and the dean is the Very Rev. Edward Craig Maclure, D.D. The cathedral in its present form dates only from a comparatively recent period and, except a portion of the walls, there is very little left of the edifice as it stood in the days of Henry VII. The beautiful tower, which is an almost exact reproduc-

F. Frith & Co.] THE CATHEDRAL. *[Reigate.*

tion of the old one, but in better material, is new from foundation to pinnacles. New mullions have been put in the windows, many of which have been refilled with stained glass. New choir stalls have been erected, a new reredos has been set up, and a large amount of tasteful and ornamental work well carried out. Altogether something like £60,000 has been expended on the restoration and beautifying of the "Old Church," including the new tower, which was completed in 1868. Of this large sum at least £23,000 has been laid out within the last few years, and the results have been highly satisfactory, the cathedral being now in a condition worthy of so great and wealthy a diocese, though it must be said that a still larger and more magnificent edifice would accord better with the status and position of modern Manchester.

Of the Assize Courts it may truly be said that they are not surpassed in the kingdom for comfort, commodiousness, and excellent arrangement. Certainly, in no other courts that we have seen is there such ample provision for the accommodation of the public, as well as for the convenience of all persons having business to transact. The building consists of a centre, with two wings, and is externally about 250 feet long by 150 feet deep. The architectural effect is greatly enhanced by the wise liberality of the Corporation, who have left an open space of more than 100 feet in depth in front of the building.

F. Frith & Co.] MANCHESTER ASSIZE COURTS. [Reigate.

The Town Hall is one of the most superb structures for the transaction of municipal business to be met with in any part of the world, and was built to replace the somewhat confined and inconvenient buildings in King Street. It was opened in 1876, and represents one of the noblest results of the policy of improvement so long and so effectively pursued by the modern "city fathers."

F. Frith & Co.]   THE TOWN HALL.   [Reigate.

CHAPTER III.

GROWTH OF MANCHESTER
AND
DEVELOPMENT OF COTTON INDUSTRY
DURING THE NINETEENTH CENTURY.

DURING the nineteenth century, the manifold developments in the methods of production, the means of distribution, and the facilities for intercommunication, have been so numerous as to prevent the possibility of a further description than a brief summary of the influences which, during the nine decades of this century, have combined to make Manchester the next community in rank to London in its metropolitan qualifications Among these influences were the interesting labours of Richard Trevethick, John Blenkinsop, William Hedley, and Timothy Hackworth, which, with the great triumph of George Stephenson—the construction of the Liverpool and Manchester Railway—initiated an era of unexampled progress, which has extended over a period exceeding half a century.

Simultaneously with the efforts of the persistent and ingenious minds which had so vastly improved methods of production and distribution, enlightened statesmen had devoted their energies to the deletion from our statutes of some of the impolitic restrictions which had seriously hampered the legitimate progress of industrial development. These legislative reforms have greatly contributed to the expansion of our world-wide commerce. Every agency which lessens the difficulties opposed to the intercommunication of mankind helps by so much the general progress of the human race. In the enormous development of the interests of this country generally, and of Manchester interests particularly, the varied applications of the electric telegraph, and the postal reforms initiated by Sir Rowland Hill, have contributed in an immeasurable degree. The combined operation of mechanical improvements, the inception of ocean steam navigation, scientific research, moral reforms, and improved means of internal communication, have each played a material part in the developments which have made Manchester the greatest workshop of the world, and the commercial metropolis of a population as great as that of Holland and Belgium combined, inhabiting a considerably less area than those countries taken together. No better register of the growth of Manchester can be found than the following figures exhibiting the increase of the commerce of Liverpool, which is simply a reflex of the prosperity of the great industrial area of which Manchester is the commercial emporium.

THE DEVELOPMENT OF LIVERPOOL COMMERCE.

Year.	Number of vessels.	Aggregate tonnage of vessels.	Mean tonnage.	Dock rates and town dues.
1801	5,060	459,719	98	£28,365
1811	5,616	611,190	109	54,752
1821	7,810	839,848	113	94,556
1831	12,537	1,592,436	127	183,455
1841	16,108	2,425,461	150	175,506
1851	21,071	3,737,666	177	246,686
1861	21,095	4,977,272	236	611,006
1871	20,121	6,131,745	305	789,031
1881	20,249	7,893,948	390	966,281
1889	22,662	9,291,964	410	990,552*

The Customs tonnage returns for the year 1889 are—inward, 8,586,381 tons; outward, 8,307,442 tons; total, 16,893,823 tons; number of vessels entered and clearing, 43,443. The weight of the traffic carried would amount to 20,000,000 tons approximately.

The expansion of Manchester during the sixty years of the railway era, which had its inception in a practicable sense by the opening of the first Liverpool and Manchester railway, on September 15th, 1830, has been truly remarkable. This is evidenced by the subjoined figures, giving the accretion of population

---

* The small increase in the amount of revenue, as compared with the marked increase in the volume of tonnage, is referable to reductions in the port charges made by the Mersey Docks and Harbour Board, these reductions being mainly attributable to the moral influence of the Manchester Ship Canal having been made since the inception of the movement in 1882.

in the five poor-law districts of Manchester, Chorlton, Salford, Barton, and Prestwich, which constitute in the aggregate one homogeneous community. The figures are taken from the census returns made for the respective periods:—

1831.	1851.	1871.	1891.
284,238	471,332	643,801	954,808

The progress of our nation in wealth and commercial prosperity during the last fifty years is marvellous. The population has increased by eleven and a-half millions; the imports of the country have increased by £300,000,000; the revenue has gone up from £55,000,000 to £90,000,000; and, as was proved in the evidence of the Manchester Ship Canal advocates, the shipping has advanced from nine million tons to more than sixty million tons. The postage has made perhaps the most extraordinary leaps, having now reached the prodigious figures: one thousand five hundred million letters annually, five thousand million newspapers and books, one thousand eight hundred million post cards. The income of the country has risen to over £600,000,000, and is still increasing, which in itself shows how greatly our command of the comforts and conveniences of life has increased. This is true as much, if not more, of the labouring population as of the middle and higher classes. The wider distribution of wealth, the cheapness of food and clothing, better and more general éducation, have all tended to bring within the reach of every class comforts and enjoyments undreamed of before; increased longevity is one of the most marked results, as may be seen from our insurance office statistics.

Manchester has admittedly played its part in the general progress. When the writer came to the town in 1845, the population of Manchester was not more than two hundred and fifty thousand, and that of Salford about fifty thousand. In both boroughs the growth has been remarkable, but especially in what is now known as greater Manchester, which takes in the population within a radius of four miles from the Royal Exchange, which is mainly, one might almost say entirely, dependent upon Manchester. The population of this wider area is over eight hundred thousand, and is constantly increasing.

About the time referred to (1845) Messrs. James Brown, Son, and Co., were in Cannon Street; Messrs. S. and J. Watts and Co., in Fountain Street; Messrs. E. and J. Jackson, in Mosley Street, at the corner of York Street, where the noble edifice belonging to the Manchester and Salford Banking Company now stands. At the opposite corner stood the old and well-known linen house of Blackwell's. The latter left the trade, but Messrs. Jackson occupied for some time the substantial building next to the Queen's Hotel, now in the occupation of the well-known firm of Richardson, Tee, and Rycroft. Messrs. Kershaw,

Lees, and Co., occupied the adjoining warehouse, having removed from the building they had so long occupied in High Street. Messrs. Barbour Bros., having built their palatial warehouse in Aytoun Street, left their old premises corner of Aytoun Street and Portland Street, which Messrs. J. F. and H. Roberts purchased, erecting on the site the substantial structure they have since occupied. Within a short period of the time we refer to, Portland Street had been occupied very largely by a poor class of property. But shortly after this date it rose in character almost at a bound, and has become a great centre of the commercial power of our city and has in it properties which would be a credit to any town.

High Street is another thoroughfare which has considerably improved, and, in addition to the three piles of buildings occupied by Rylands and Sons, Limited, it has in it other enterprising firms, and the future of this street will be greater than the past.

Some large houses have continued to develop on and around the ground they have for many years occupied in Church Street. This street is still improving in style of buildings, but there is room for further progress in this direction. The writer hopes to live to see the time when the whole length of the street, from High Street to Ducie Street, will be known as Church Street, and will be occupied by strong concerns, which will do their share in the further development of this vast centre for the distribution of the varied and ever-increasing manufactures of Lancashire and Yorkshire.

Another item is noteworthy, the change in our city architecture generally being characterised by great improvements. One would specially enumerate among these the palatial Town Hall, the Assize Courts, the Royal Exchange, the General Post Office in Spring Gardens, which ranks next in the magnitude of its business to that of St. Martin's-le-Grand in the metropolis, and includes in its function the postal economy of over one hundred towns; the Owens' College, the seat of the Victoria University, the Grammar School, the Exchange Station, the magnificent warehouses, and most recently numerous new insurance and bank buildings. These all have done much to elevate the character of the city, and impart to it a picturesqueness which makes it attractive to visitors from a distance, and a joy to those of us who are proud to call ourselves citizens of Manchester. The improvement in the Consolidated Bank Buildings, the erection of the new National Provincial Bank in York Street, Manchester and County, Manchester Joint Stock, and the Lancashire and Yorkshire Banks have added greatly to the architecture of King Street, and indeed we might say of the city.

The story of the development of a great town is always interesting and sometimes very remarkable. Conversation with an old inhabitant frequently affords both amusement and instruction. One is urged to reflect what circumstances have caused the current of trade to flow in this or in that direction ; why the land in one thoroughfare should be valued at £30 or £50 per yard, whilst in another street, which at a period one can remember would have been considered by many shrewd people as one of the best investments for the future, it has actually gone down in value; why one side of a thoroughfare is so much more valuable than the other, so that, in some instances, a moderate shop worth £300 on one side of the street will be worth £500 or more directly opposite. Or, again, taking a given locality that is purely residential, but where by the increase of population a necessity has arisen for shops, why does this or that street take the preference apart altogether from any desire or opinion of the landlord? It is interesting, too, to notice how the extension of business premises over a wider area diminishes the value of house property up to a certain point, which we will call the middle of the three zones in which the property of a city is situate, so that houses formerly let at £80 and £100 per annum fall in value till it becomes difficult to let them at £30 or £40; but, in the course of fifteen or twenty years, as the trade continues to grow, this property rises again in value, being occupied for manufacturing purposes or for sale-rooms, and so recoups in large measure, if not fully, all past losses.

But citizens of our "no mean city" have grounds for rejoicing in its prosperity not simply as regards its commercial importance, but also in its moral, intellectual, and legal aspects. There is no need to dwell upon the many philanthropic and kindly influences at work in our midst. The support given to hospitals, to children's homes and refuges, and to home and foreign missions, tells of many who are striving each to fill the niche prepared for him in the scheme of the world's uplifting.

The movement for the education of the people has taken a deep hold of the sympathies of our citizens, and our city has assumed a status in the educational world second only to London and the ever-famous centres, Oxford and Cambridge. Our own university and colleges, schools of the higher grade for men and women, together with our public and board schools, are producing a change within all classes of society, which will have a marked influence in all the varied relations of our people. We have taken rank amongst the largest cities in the empire as a publishing centre, being exceeded in this particular only by Edinburgh and London.

In medicine we stand high, and in the musical world only London outshines us.

Our activity in legal matters will be touched upon in a later chapter.

With reference to municipal administration, it needs but little argument to enforce the truth of the statement that economy is easier in a larger than in a smaller town. With the administrative ability that a large corporation like Greater Manchester would furnish, supplying gas, water, and public baths, and maintaining streets, sewage, and police, under the management of the various committees, saving would be effected and advantages enjoyed which the writer believes it impossible for minor local authorities to secure. To those who are familiar with the management of large concerns, it will be well known that a manager with twenty assistants under him can, by virtue of his developed capacity and extended experience, as easily direct forty as twenty men; so, too, in the collection of accounts, in the purchase of land, the laying out of a new district in the neighbourhood of new railways or a ship canal, and in a thousand and one ways, concentrated action would be both more economical and more effective. The writer has for a long time been an advocate of the amalgamation into one municipality of the whole district and population within a four-mile radius from the Manchester Royal Exchange. All the people within that radius practically depend upon the business earnings of the city, and this is especially the case in the borough of Salford and the district of Moss Side, the two places which resolutely refuse to join Manchester on grounds of economy.

CHAPTER IV.

MANCHESTER HOME-TRADE HOUSES.

THERE has been much discussion and correspondence of late as to the wholesale home-trader's prospects in Manchester. "An exodus of merchant houses, such as was never seen before," characterises the last few years in the opinion of "Manchester Man," writing to the *Drapers' Record*. He says, the effect of a walk round the Infirmary is saddening: "To let," or "This warehouse will be divided to suit tenants," meets the eye at every turn. Another says, what is again and again being reported, that "the old houses have ceased to exist, and the trade is being absorbed by others." And again, "the merchant must cease and only the manufacturer remain; all the old landmarks of the town will be removed." The same facts are referred to in an able letter to the *Manchester City News* of November 3rd, 1888. The correspondent says: "During late years an undue proportion of the wholesale home-trade houses, old and young firms, have gone out of business or come to grief, and of those existing now, a few only have increased their trade considerably. . . . The change has been more of an epidemic character than one of isolated cases of disease. It has carried off old and young alike." In three articles in the *City News*, of dates November 24th, December 1st, and December 8th, 1888, the same facts are re-stated: "That Manchester is rapidly losing her supremacy as a distributing centre will hardly be denied. The purchasing power of the people has increased largely during the past thirty years, but our home trade has certainly not increased in the same ratio. On the contrary, appearances indicate retrogression. Drapers from outlying districts do not come to Manchester in the numbers or with the frequency of former days. The fancy trade is gravitating to London, and, unfortunately for us, the heavy trade appears likely to follow. The provincial wholesale houses, who now go, as far as possible, direct to manufacturers, are becoming more formidable competitors, and are yearly securing a larger share of the trade."

Now, to the writer the aspect of business matters is decidedly more cheerful, and our home trade offers a vastly better prospect for rising and industrious young men in the future than some of the extracts quoted imply. When the writer was a young man he, too, was accustomed to see the old and honoured names in Cannon Street, High Street, Church Street, Fountain Street, Piccadilly, and latterly in Dale Street, Portland Street, Parker Street, York Street, and Mosley Street;

to many of which reference was made in the last chapter. These localities are to-day largely occupied by what are known as the home-trade houses, firms which at the present time have little or no connection with the foreign or colonial trade. General shipping houses are spread all over the district within three-quarters of a mile from the Infirmary; but there is no need in the present connection to make any particular reference to the shipping houses as such, except to say that they have immensely increased during the past twenty years, alike in number, importance, and reputation, and now cover with their palatial buildings the most important parts of our city, and employ directly and indirectly a very large portion of the population in and around the city.

Returning to the home-trade houses, reference has been made to the decay and removal of old and respected firms. It would be as well, instead of dwelling upon these changes, to look at the number of rising firms that are to be found in the fancy trade, the ready-made clothes, boots and shoes, and the mantle trade, many of whom bid fair to rival, in the extent of business and wealth, if not to excel, the magnates of the past. In the list of new concerns, mention should be made of the great co-operative institution in Balloon Street, Manchester. The writer ventures to say that the turnover in the houses now existing will be found to exceed by some millions of pounds sterling the returns made by the firms in the good old times; and if the men of the present day were as unostentatious, as attentive, and as industrious as the men of the past generation, there would be a still larger and more satisfactory business done. Referring to a letter of the present writer in the same issue, a leader in the *City News* of October 27th, 1888, says: "Our correspondent is right when he says that substantial reasons can be given for the disappearance of most old concerns. It is a mistake to imagine that old firms disappear from no fault of their own. Failure in either an old or new concern is due in both alike to inherent weakness. Nobody supposes that old concerns are thrown into the shade or compelled to retire when they have the same capital, business capacity, and energy as their new rivals. Surely, if the latter can hold their own, the former, with their old connection, should be able to do so likewise. In business, as in everything else, it is the fittest which survives. Unless old concerns adapt themselves to their continually changing environment, it is impossible for them to survive. And why should they? Why should old firms be maintained by props of prejudice, custom, or sentimental sympathies? These supports will never be of much use for any length of time to a house struggling with a host of competitors. Those firms prosper most which serve their customers best. If a house will not spend money wisely in developing its business, then its trade will go to other concerns which comply with this requirement. If it refuses to deal liberally with its customers, its customers will go where they are dealt with liberally. If the partners in a concern are too big to welcome their customers, the latter will find a welcome elsewhere. If principals do not take an active part in superintending the various departments of their business, nor in encouraging the enterprise and energy of those under them, they will soon find themselves below those who do. If capital is withdrawn by old partners and not replaced by new ones, it is unwise to carry on business in the same extensive way; and, if it is attempted to do so, success is not possible. If we regret the ill success of some old firms, should we not rejoice at the progress of others and at the growth of new ones ? Why should not the new men have our sympathy in their struggle, and our admiration at their success ? Business cannot stand still. It must either go backwards or forwards. The fact that all the rewards of business are not confined to a set of old concerns is a stimulus to the energy of every new comer. The progress of many concerns testifies that if people adapt themselves to the wants of the day, and pursue their avocations with intelligence and energy, there is yet room for prosperity."

It must be borne in mind that the textile and kindred trades are very varied in their character, and employ the highest talent we can find amongst designers, artists, and manufacturers. It is difficult, nay it is impossible, for any one to measure the possibilities in the different branches of these businesses, between the plain article which satisfies the tastes and desires of the West Indian coolie or the natives of Iceland, to the beautiful and artistic article of dress which would suit the taste of the young ladies of our city. There is room to employ a diversity of talent in the workshop, the mill, and the Manchester warehouse, which latter is the saleroom for their various products. The writer ventures to say that the skill and capacity of individuals engaged in producing goods for the home-trade houses have yet ample space for development, and that, instead of there being fewer warehouses wanted, there should be more.

Take, for instance, the fancy business as understood in the home trade. This has not by any means secured the high position which the population of the North of England warrants. Then the ready-made trade, the boot and shoe trade, though there are some enterprising firms in these branches in the city, no one will say they fully meet the buying powers of the business men who visit this market. They also can be still further and largely developed. The same remarks apply to the mantle trade, a business which requires great skill and ingenuity, and which is yet in its infancy. Then, the carpet and furnishing business. This is a large and ever-increasing branch, but is neglected in this city.

The writer would call the attention of manufacturers to the want of more novel and beautiful designs in counterpanes and quilts. In eider-downs the development has been wonderful, and met with the success which the artistic taste displayed has well merited. Strange, while all other goods used in domestic furnishing have been improving in design, style, and utility, quilts have not received the attention which an article of such large consumption demands, and which it would pay to bestow. We hear from the Black Country of great progress in the products of the sheet-iron makers; that they are able to make sheets so fine and pure, and capable of being folded, that addresses presented to Mr. Gladstone were written upon them. Is there any genius amongst the sheet and quilt manufacturers of this manufacturing district who can strike out a new idea, and develop this vast industry, bringing beauty and attractiveness of design into an article of such constant and all-round service ?

Notwithstanding the possibilities of further progress and development in different branches, any person who will count up the comparatively new but successful firms, which are to be found in the locality occupied by home-trade houses, will find cause for rejoicing rather than sadness. The extreme, and one might say interesting, variety of goods, which are sold in our various warehouses, will employ a great diversity of skilled labour, and capable men as masters and servants. It is not possible for any half dozen firms to meet the wants of traders and their customers, the millions who populate England and her colonies.

Let us dwell for a moment upon the variety of goods which are sold to-day in home-trade warehouses. Formerly, any of us wanting a coat or a suit of clothes went to the woollen draper, and bought the needed quantity of cloth, then took it to the tailor to be made up. If we or our wives and children wanted a pair of boots, we went to get measured at the shoemaker's. If we wanted a bag, a purse, or fancy article, they had to be sought away altogether from the draper, and still more, if an article of furniture was required for our home, the cabinet-maker must be visited. All this is altered. Stocks of all these goods can now be found on the premises of our large drapers, and yet we find most of the large wholesale houses in the city jogging along on the old lines. Why do they not follow the changed habits and conditions of modern life, and provide, so far as their means will allow, what is required by their clients? If any one asks, "Where will you draw the line?" the writer would reply, "In dry goods." Any articles—excepting, of course, such bulky articles as coals—which can be required by man, woman, or child, from birth to death, for their persons or their homes, should be supplied, but not soft goods, that is, provisions. We may rest assured that there will always be a large number of merchants required to conduct so large and varied a business. The centres of textile manufacturing industry, which *must* be visited by the wholesale buyers of our warehouses, exist in various parts of our own country, in Scotland, Ireland, and Wales, and also in Germany, France, Italy, Switzerland, Austria, and Russia. The goods selected from all these centres, together with the articles of our own manufacture, are distributed from Manchester over the whole of Britain, our colonies, and to the continents of Europe and America—we may say the world. The great and almost immeasurable diversity of taste and culture, and the corresponding variety of requirements to be found within so wide an area of distribution, will necessitate a large number of distributors, who possess capital and ability—men and women who carefully study the wants of their clients, and who can stock their warehouses with suitable materials for meeting their demands. It is absurd to say, as some do, that the trade will be swallowed by a few houses. Of course, the best-managed houses, and the most capable and industrious men who have capital, will rise above others, and secure a larger trade. But that three or six men or firms in Manchester do or ever can possess all the genius and force necessary to absorb and conduct the whole of the textile branch, and satisfy the tastes of the thirty thousand to fifty thousand merchants and drapers, who deal with Manchester houses, is beyond any intelligent man's belief. Take, for instance, mantles, ready-mades, furniture, prints, haberdashery, fancy goods, or almost any branch : a moment's reflection will show that there is both room and need for a large number of merchants and general dealers, persons or firms, who devote themselves to one, two, or three special articles, apart altogether from the manufacturers. There are at present forty thousand commercial travellers. Now, suppose that, instead of these travellers working from given distributing centres, the whole of the manufacturers from Leicester, Nottingham, Derby, Northampton, Loughborough, Hinckley, Belper, Luton, London, Bolton, Bury, Wigan, Preston, Colne, Clitheroe, Blackburn, Haslingden, Bacup, Accrington, Heywood, Rochdale, Hebden Bridge, Halifax, Bradford, Dewsbury, Batley, Huddersfield, Leeds, Wakefield, Barnsley, Heckmondwike, Sowerby Bridge, Todmorden, Stockport, Ashton, Denton, and a score of other towns in this country, where textile goods are made, together with towns in Scotland, Ireland, and Wales, as well as in the numerous continental centres of textile manufacture,—let us suppose that all these were to send their own travellers to the drapers in the cities and towns of this, not to say of other countries, the loss of time and the annoyance to the retail trader would only be exceeded in foolish impracticability by the wasteful expenditure that would be incurred, and for which the people, the real consumers, must pay.

The reader will thus see the necessity there is for

wholesale warehouses and fixed centres for distribution. They must exist; and, for economy in time, labour, and expense, the fewer general centres the better. The writer, for one, believes there are men possessing the requisite talent, if they had the confidence, to establish new departments and new firms or companies, and that the enlargement which has taken place within the past few years is but the beginning of greater and better things for Manchester. Men who begin now will be free from the demoralising influence attending the prosperity of 1862 and 1870 to 1874, which stifled the energy and almost destroyed the ability that had up to that date made Manchester merchants and manufacturers the best-known and respected men in the country. The high prices which ruled during the American war, followed as it was so quickly by the Franco-German war, started traders in habits of living, lifted them and many of their men into spheres or positions, from which it is hard to descend. Many date their trade troubles from those periods. Long may it be before such a time of commercial demoralisation is experienced again.

There can be no doubt that all the suffering referred to by other writers has been greatly aggravated and intensified by the great depression in our agricultural districts. This, however, seems now to be giving place to better times. Our farmers are more hopeful and buoyant, and certainly many branches of industry throughout the midland and northern counties are improving. There is more hope and confidence, and better profits all round are to be expected.

Further, if the outlook from the present aspect of business matters were as dark as some would picture it, what is the answer to the question of fact that several of the largest concerns have so greatly increased their business and the size of their premises? They are labouring in the same neighbourhood, breathe the same atmosphere, buy in the same markets, and they are not sons of that man of great stature, named in the Book of Chronicles, whose fingers and toes were four-and-twenty—six on each hand and six on each foot. "No one," says the writer of the leader in the *City News*, already quoted, "surely will venture on the bold statement that new concerns prosper by reason of adopting improper business methods. If improper business practices injure the old concerns, how can it be imagined that the same practices will not injure the new concerns? Is it not to be feared that new departures which men make in business, because of their foreseeing likely changes amongst customers, are often described without reason as unsound or unfair methods? Many of them are nothing of the kind, and this is seen by the fact that departures at first denounced become in a short time very general, and at last the prevailing custom. If the men who were once the chief warehousemen in Manchester were to look to-day into some of the large Manchester warehouses, they would be simply bewildered at the enormous number of articles dealt in, many of which were, in their day, foreign to their business; some did not even exist. It is more than probable that those gentlemen would not hold the position they once had in business if they lived now and adhered to their old principles and modes of working. . . . During the past twenty years, coincidently with the change that has been taking place in the wholesale and retail drapery houses at home, hundreds of thousands of our countrymen—English, Irish, Scotch, and Welsh—have gone out to the different countries abroad. They have taken British notions, British industry, and business capacity with them to the East and West Indies, to America, Canada, Scandinavia, to Africa, South America, and some parts of China. They are trading on much the same lines that are being followed in this country; many of them come over to England to buy their wares just as regularly and even more frequently than our customers from remote parts of our own land. And yet, with a few notable exceptions, amongst the home-trade houses they fail to find the goods required for their various markets, notwithstanding that Manchester is the centre of our various industries. It is notorious that the colonial trade is the backbone of the Glasgow home-trade houses. Taken all round, the colonial business is the most rapidly increasing and prosperous that England possesses, and the goods used are the reflex of what are sold in the home-trade. There was, therefore, no reason why Manchester, had she exerted herself, might not have had a larger share of this trade."

Assuredly, commercial wisdom does not reside in apathy, or in holding aloof from the demands which the altered conditions of trading impose. The fact of "a modern drapery establishment bearing a greater resemblance to an American dry goods store than to an old English shop" should in itself decide the course for the wholesale trader to adopt. The house that suits itself to the draper's requirements will naturally secure his custom. Why should not this be true of the Manchester wholesale houses? Situated in the very heart of the most important manufacturing district in the world, whose products are in universal demand—and with the extension of civilisation an increasing demand—Manchester is and must be the great centre for distribution. Within a radius of forty miles of the Manchester Exchange we have seven millions of people, and when Salford realises the importance of her amalgamation with Manchester, and the accruing advantages begin to be felt, then, as the centre of this vast population and the second city in the empire, we shall, if the home-trade houses will rise to the position and the opportunity, take our proper place as a trading community. Our facilities for producing, arising from our easy access to coal and iron, the nerve and sinew of manufacture, and for distributing, arising from our central position, should not only encourage the further development of existing firms, but be an incentive to energetic young men who desire to make their mark and to rank amongst the merchants of our city. The modern facilities for travelling enable our buyers to visit any market, at home or abroad, on equal terms with buyers from any other place in the kingdom; and the construction of the Manchester Ship Canal will give us still further advantages in this respect; cotton, wool, and other raw materials will soon be laid almost at our mill doors from the vessels which bring them from all parts of the world.

The importance of the Ship Canal to Manchester as a trading centre it would be difficult to exaggerate. The very fact of the passing of the Act, "after the most prolonged struggle in the history of private Bill legislation," speaks for itself. The commercial evidence before six committees of the two Houses of Parliament was so convincing as to secure the verdict of the most competent men in Westminster in its favour. The importance to the future trade of the country of opening up direct intercourse between the centre of such large manufacturing and mercantile operations and other nations was clearly recognised, and should be recognised by all who are interested in the future of Manchester as a trading centre. The effect of the inland water-carriage will be to facilitate and cheapen the moving of raw materials—cotton, corn, timber, wool, fur, &c., which, being bulky, have seriously suffered from the burden of the railway charges. Great loss of time in transhipping and extra expense result from unloading in Liverpool goods for the greater part of which Manchester is the natural centre of distribution. The continuation of the ocean voyage of a vessel a few hours' steam inland is so inappreciable in relation to the whole distance traversed, that vessels would only require the same freight to Manchester as required to Liverpool. An illustration is given by the parallel case of Havre, at the mouth of the Seine, and Rouen, sixty miles on that river above Havre, the freight of ocean-going vessels to either port being equal. This clearly does away with the whole cost of the railway carriage between Liverpool and Manchester. Owing to this important fact, the maximum tariff fixed by the Manchester Ship Canal Act, 1885, which the company may charge, is fixed at exactly one-half of the combined port and railway charges as they stood at the time the Act was obtained, in other words, a reduction of fifty per cent. With these increased facilities trade will naturally expand; the volume of traffic will be greater; and the railways, and even Liverpool itself, will not be injured, but benefited. There is no doubt that we have suffered severely from the effects of the high rates of transit, both import and export.

For years past everything has been done to reduce the cost of production ; the energies of the proprietors of our various manufactories have been devoted to this end in the speeding and development of machine power, the reduction of wages, and of general standing expenses. Every decrease in the cost of production to the manufacturer means, in the long run, increased ability for the trader buying from him to compete in home or foreign markets. When the Canal is in active operation, we shall be materially helped in our efforts to contend with strong competitors in foreign markets by the minimising of the charges for carriage to the sea. There is every probability, too, that ships, which now load exclusively in London, will come up to Manchester, part loaded, to complete their cargoes, in the same way that ships now load partially in Glasgow and fill up at Liverpool. This will again effect a very large saving, which will tell in favour both of manufacturers and merchants in the race of competition.

Moreover, what is to prevent a large business coming through the port of Manchester from Huddersfield, Batley, Dewsbury, Leeds, Sheffield, the Potteries, and Birmingham district, and from the coalfields of Lancashire, South Yorkshire, and North Staffordshire ? In that case not only would Manchester be benefited, but the industries of these districts would be largely developed. The establishment of works along the banks of the new Canal cannot fail to add to our prosperity. It was the prospect of this new field of labour for the increasing population that largely helped to secure the sympathy and gain the strong and hearty approbation of the industrial classes of this city and district. It was the deep immovable conviction that the sons and daughters of the present generation would have a future in their own country, and not the outlook of a miserable pittance here or life on a foreign and unknown shore, that led fifty thousand men to assemble on common ground on Saturday, June 21st, 1884, to say, so far as their means and strength could say, that the Canal should be made. The writer will not forget a working man coming up to him after one of the many meetings he attended in support of the scheme, who addressed him by name, and said, "God bless you, and all the other gentlemen that are working so hard in this great scheme! It will do us all good, and our children, too." It was but the voice of thousands, who thought and felt as he did, but did not express it in the same homely way.

With the immediate prospect on the completion of the Canal of saving Lancashire alone more than £1,000,000 per annum; with a present business aspect not by any means so gloomy as some would picture it; with the opening up of new industries on and around the Canal, is there not every likelihood of improved business in every department? With industries localised around us, a population born and reared under the noise of loom and spindle, inhaling the atmosphere of bleach and dye works, learning from earliest life to manipulate the raw materials, driven not only by the necessities of family life, but also by what might be called an industrial instinct, to an acquaintance with the various processes of manufacturing and finishing goods, so that in mechanism, in experience, and in habits of industry the population of this district is not excelled in this or in any country in the world, we have a right to say that this is and ought to be a grand centre for mercantile operations, and to look forward to our future with hope and confidence.

Returning to the business of the warehouse, so far nothing has been said on the subject of dating forward. It is a vexed question, and a brief statement of opinion, with the reasons for it, is all that would be in place here. As the reader will know, there are many, including the correspondent, "Manchester Man," already referred to, who trace all the troubles of the home trade to this source. "The merchants here have never recognised the force of the fact that there is a competition of terms as well as of prices, and that the former is often the greater factor of the two." "Town Traveller," in the issue of May 11th, 1889 (*Drapers' Record*), says, "The dating-forward system is increasing amongst the London houses and that continuously. I venture the opinion that until Manchester and other centres adopt the same system, nearly all the buyers, especially those who do their own counting-house work, will favour the London houses." A "South of England Draper," writing in the next issue, May 17th, is of the same opinion: "The 'dating forward' may be a rotten system, I am not arguing on that, but as long as it is a recognised system of the trade, as it now is, and Manchester refuses to recognise it, so long will Manchester have cause to complain of the transition of its trade."

The practice indicated as necessary to the salvation of the Manchester home trade is the giving of two or three months' extra credit on special occasions. The slowness of Manchester wholesale houses to adopt this practice is said to account for the progress other firms are making in competing with them for the draper's custom. Now, long experience and observation have convinced the writer that the drapers are amongst the shrewdest and most capable traders in the country, and the best of them, who have means and are judges of the goods they buy, will not be long in finding out the different values offered by the various houses. All intelligent men in the wholesale trade know pretty nearly the average profit, and can, therefore, say whether it is paying a house to sell at the ordinary profit, and give other facilities which they cannot afford. Extra dating and discount must be made up in price, and the safest and most reliable men know this and buy accordingly. It would be well for every house to decline dating forward any plain cotton goods, which have to be paid for quickly, and on which there is a very small margin of profit, a fact well known to all buyers. Dating of season goods and an exceptional sale are necessities for which all can make allowance.

The evils of the system, in the view of the writer, can be best illustrated by an example. Suppose a respectable young firm, wholesale, does £120,000 per annum. One extra month's terms means a further credit of £10,000 in their books. This capital cannot be added in the year from profits, and must therefore be borrowed, or the time given must be brought back by an extra discount for cash or bills, or it must be taken from the manufacturer in extended terms under certain conditions; this means at least full one-half per cent. loss, or addition to expenses; and this is not all, as we will presently show. Now, the wholesale trade is competed for so keenly that a difference like this takes a very important part of the profit. What is the inevitable result? Naturally, the expenses being increased the price must be raised to recoup the loss. But a trader replies, "Few men can tell to one-half or one per cent." Yes, but this is not all. The merchant finds that a number of unscrupulous traders have started business in various towns. The fact of their taking the extra time is not the whole nor the end of the evil. The trade of the place in which they have commenced business will only support a certain number of dealers, and the effect often is that the old, respectable, reliable customer of many years' standing is so beaten in the race that he fails, and the wholesale house has to accept ten shillings in the pound. Or, if the old trader is too strong and beats his new rival, which frequently happens, then the last comer succumbs; but, instead of receiving ten shillings in the pound, you find his trading has all been on the capital of the creditor. He has little or no capital of his own, and when the winding-up comes under an assignment, it is five shillings, or, if in the court, perhaps three shillings or three shillings and sixpence. Taking in these losses, there is a larger percentage to be added to expenses. The trader would find, by analysing the facts, that he has to pay more than one-half or one per cent. for the gratification of his desire for dating forward. It is a pernicious system whichever way one looks at it, and is productive of untold trouble and evil to wholesale and retail traders alike.

Chapter V.

RETAIL TRADE IN MANCHESTER GOODS.

RETAIL TRADERS.

THE writer does not believe that any fixed plans and regulations can, of themselves, make a man successful, but if he has intelligence, industry, and tact, combined with a technical knowledge of the various goods he buys, and the necessary capital, then method and rules will help him. He will see for himself the importance of following certain fixed principles.

As to his stock, the character of it must depend upon the town and the district in which he is located. The size or value of his stock will depend largely upon the population he has to work upon. If he is in a large town of more than two hundred thousand people, he needs a less stock in proportion to his turnover than he would in a smaller town; in fact, the result of experience is proof to the writer that from the small place, say of two thousand inhabitants, where the trader has to keep almost everything, to the city of half a million of people, the average stock will vary from twelve weeks' turnover in the larger town to thirty or thirty-six weeks' turnover in the smaller. The following statement may be taken as a guide: in towns of from two thousand to five thousand inhabitants, a draper may hold a stock equal to thirty to thirty-six weeks' turnover; in towns of from five thousand to ten thousand inhabitants twenty-six to thirty weeks' turnover.

10,000 to	20,000 inhabitants,	24 to 26 weeks' turnover.		
20,000 to	50,000	,,	20 to 24	,, ,,
50,000 to	100,000	,,	20 to 22	,, ,,
100,000 to	200,000	,,	18 to 20	,, ,,
200,000 and upwards		,,	16 to 20	,, ,,

When this population is reached (two hundred thousand and upwards) it greatly depends upon the head of the business as to the amount and character of the stock he keeps. If he decides upon keeping rich and valuable goods, together with carpets and woollens, then the proportion changes.

One matter is of the utmost importance to all small traders. Fresh and clean stock is essential to prosperity. The increased expense of carriage, caused by more frequent purchases, whether at the wholesale house or through the travellers, will be far more than counterbalanced by the smaller stock that is required to be kept, and the quicker payment of accounts that can be made, thereby saving discount. The old habit of buying largely twice a year has quite gone out of fashion; smart, successful drapers are buying or ordering weekly, many daily. The great variety of fancy goods—new things being constantly brought into the market—makes it a necessity to be always ready to take up new productions. This cannot be done if the stock is filled up. The great danger is of buying too much, especially in these times when credit is so cheap and parcels are continually being dated forward. Young tradesmen often get the impression, when they buy on forward date, that the pay day is so far ahead that no disaster can occur; but they find very soon to their cost that dated goods are not only not the cheapest, but that the due date of their bills comes much sooner than they expected. Repeatedly, when being interviewed, young men give their liabilities at, say, £1,200, omitting altogether dated-forward parcels, which, when added, bring up the amount to £1,500 or £1,600. If traders, in addition to the above regulations as to the amount of stock they should hold on an average, would lay down the following golden rule, they would be benefited to an extent they cannot at present comprehend; only experience can sufficiently impress their minds with its importance. Assuming that a trader is doing for the most part a cash trade, he should *never allow his liabilities to trade creditors to exceed two to two and a-half-times his capital.*

If a tradesman's capital is £500 and he owes £1,250, this gives a total working stock of £1,750.

On a stock of this amount he can, according to the size of the town, turn over, say, £3,500, in a large centre £4,000, or in a great population £5,000 per annum.

We will take the moderate-sized town, and say he does £4,000 per annum or about £330 per month; with this turnover he can pay in four months, that is, he can pay within net terms, and have a small margin. Before long economy in the working of his business should place him in a position to take full advantage of discounts, and of special lines and cheap parcels, which are always being placed in the way of a cash man, which but seldom reach the hands of a slow payer.

Where the draper's trade is largely on credit terms, his difficulties are greater; his capital and credit are being put largely into his books, and he has to be content with a smaller stock and a less turnover. His aim must be to restrict, so far as possible, the credit part of his business; buyers will not pay the prices they did formerly to compensate for long credits, and the various organisations for promoting cash business throughout the country are so strong that the shopkeeper must have well-ordered stocks and must sell cheaply. The tendency of legislation for some years past has been to do away with all facilities which foster the credit system, and to force people to do a cash business, and certainly the civil service, co-operative societies, &c., all help to educate the people to this system. If traders generally would more resolutely follow in the same direction great good would be effected, a healthier state of trade would exist, and less anxiety both for the retail and wholesale houses of the country.

In good times, when money is plentiful and people can afford to buy easily and freely, they do not run about so much from one place of business to another to find out the cheapest article; if they see goods they like, they buy them.

As a rule, a draper will be successful if he has a fair, all-round acquaintance with his class of goods, good taste in selection, and the ability to dress his windows attractively—a most important element in the prosperity of any retail concern.

The six points in the draper's charter are:—

1. Capital, consistent with his business requirements.
2. Well-assorted and well-kept stock.
3. Capable and obliging salesmen and assistants.
4 Well-dressed windows.
5. Untiring industry.
6. Economy in every department and good management.

The following paragraphs from the *Colonial Drapers' Journal*, on "Going into Business," are worth quoting:—

Great and ambitious designs are natural to the period of early manhood, when a limited knowledge of the business of life gives confidence and an earnest longing for future success. So the young man looks forward to the time when he will be "master in his own house," with a position in the world. Buoyed by such hopes, he collects his savings and his portion for a start upon the all-important road—the road to fortune. This is the flood-tide to the average young man ; for him there appears no other road but that which leads right on to success. He pictures to himself his saving habit and temperate disposition, that he is not afraid of any amount of hard work, and so, filled with economic principles and determinations, he looks round to see what others are doing ; seeking information of this friend or that, but, after all, it too often happens that "pictures of imagination" hide many a harsh fact, leaving hard lessons to be learnt by a trying experience.

Some people there are who, full of sympathy for the young beginner, will point to numerous instances of success with an air of confidence (as though they had been behind the scenes), detailing the wonderful gifts of this man or that, their peculiarities, and extraordinary business capacity ; and when asked about the reverse side will be just as ready to attribute this man's want of success to thoughtless extravagance, another's to reckless buying or unsteady habits, &c., and thus reasoning on the most convenient lines, these great advisers will conclude by saying, "You go to work economically and carefully, and you are bound to succeed ;" forgetting that " 'Tis not in mortals to command success." . . . To fit up a shop in a style unsuited to a neighbourhood is to ensure certain failure ; fitting and stock adapted to a low-class trade being introduced into a high-class neighbourhood will not attract, while the reverse will have the effect of frightening poor people altogether. Amongst early failures, one of the greatest causes may be included under this head—a young man goes into business from a high-class establishment, where he has been accustomed to "feather-bed trade," experience unfitting him for the rough-and-ready system which his limited capital suggests ; the whole of his arrangements are made upon the most extravagant scale ; both household and shop fittings must be in first-class style ; and so the capital is absorbed, for his "white elephants" will not realise when the quiet season comes round. Overbuying is a fearful snare to young men at the present day, although everything should warn them rather to err in the opposite direction. Fashion is entirely opposed to it.

It is always best to calculate the chances of waiting for a trade, and the daily wants which must arise in a new business ; for where a man invests his whole capital on the chance of an immense return in six months, disappointment often follows ; he finds there are hundreds of things which he has forgotten to buy.

The writer has frequently been asked, when discussing the question of expenses in the management of business, what proportion the rent of premises should bear to the total? Our opinion is that in the drapery trade in large towns, on a business of—

£15 to £25 per week,	the rent should not exceed	£40 per annum.
£25 to £35 ,,	,,	,,	£50	,,
£35 to £50 ,,	,,	,,	£60/70	,,
£50 to £70 ,,	,,	,,	£80/90	,,
£70 to £100 ,,	,,	,,	£100/120	,,

By the time the returns exceed £100 per week, the character of the business is often changed, and the rules which hold good on the smaller turnover have to be varied according to the altered, enlarged, or changed position of the premises, the character of the business, and according to the widening experience of the proprietor. Rents in smaller towns are less in proportion, but interest on the additional stock it is requisite to keep fully balances this advantage.

Chapter VI.

THE LIFE AND DUTIES OF BUSINESS MEN.

IT is a remark one frequently hears in certain society, and often made by professional men, that the life of a business man is a "hum-drum sort of existence," that little or no purpose is served by it other than that of making money. Now, this is altogether at variance with facts. There is a very wide field for thought, energy, and skill in the commercial calling, and associated with it. Trade in its manifold aspects itself affords scope for the highest capacities. It is anything but hum-drum to the intelligent man; ever fresh problems arise which must be solved, contingencies must be provided for, enterprises well directed, and losses made good. Banking, insurance, buying at value, and selling at a profit are practical matters demanding very thoughtful and skilful handling. Then the business man has his duties with various institutions established for the help of the unfortunate; there is ever present with him the moral duties of his situation, his word and example affect not only his own honour, but the lives and characters of all around him; the younger employés and apprentices have to be taught the technical niceties and mercantile principles pertaining to the soundest industrial operations; the providing of technical and general schools for the children likely to occupy spheres in the business world of the next generation is but an extension of the same duty; besides that the consideration of all public matters affecting trade directly or indirectly, such as parliamentary measures, municipal restrictions or development, are well within the sphere of the attention and in large measure of the control of business men.

Take the manufacturer as an example of these facts. A manufacturer needs to be a man of mental capacity and ingenuity; he must buy or construct machinery suitable for a certain class of work, and must maintain the same in efficient condition, but to do this requires a mind of no mean order. He must have skill and taste in devising new makes of cloth; goods must be made in new designs, which shall not only meet the taste of society, but which shall positively create taste.

The goods once made, he must find or make a market for them. Then arises the necessity for the proper man to sell the production of his looms and spindles, and immediately the way is opened up to that wide field of commercial relation which includes within its area the traders in the shires of his own country and the people of distant nations. Then steps in the question of insurance by land and sea, fire and marine insurance, and banking arrangements, to facilitate the operation of buying raw products of foreign lands, and the re-shipping of the manufactured goods. These operations of buying and selling involve the employment of capable and industrious men, both at home and abroad, of clerks and assistants who have to be familiar with the rates of exchange, as they affect his foreign trade, and with the rates for discounting in their own country. So far, we view the manufacturer in a purely commercial aspect.

But his life and life-influence cover much broader ground. He is in a position in which many depend upon him for employment, and he is familiar with the fluctuations of trade and the vicissitudes arising from times of dulness and depression in the lives of the workers; as a wise and humane leader of the people's industry, he cannot but see the need of their being helped to provide for adverse times; the various benevolent and provident societies claim his interest and support; so that in questions of maintenance, providence, and social and domestic well-being, he, in some measure almost of necessity, co-operates with those who, in his industrial operations, co-operate with him. It was entirely without affectation that such large employers of labour as Sir Titus Salt and the late Mr. John Rylands said that they felt upon their shoulders the responsibility of the lives and comforts of the thousands they employed.

True of all men, it is specially true of the business man who comes into close and hourly contact with so many, that "no man liveth unto himself." Every man is influenced by the stronger mind as unfailingly as the needle by the magnet; the presence of the weakest has its weight. On all sides we are touching our fellow-beings, and they are affected for good or evil by what we are, by what we say and do, even by what we think and feel. Some are built up and strengthened by the unconscious force and influence of others, others are wrenched out of their places and thrown down. Only by strictest integrity, by habits of personal industry and punctuality, can an influence for good be assured. The order and regularity of the work in a large factory or warehouse, the quiet intelligence with which the whole is conducted, reflect the character of the head of the whole and of the several departments. If a man takes care of his character, his personal influence will take care of itself.

Were business men not predisposed to take in hand the question of general and technical education, the force of circumstances would make it imperative. The competition of the manufacturers of foreign countries, combined with the rapidly developing tastes and corresponding demands of the people, alike force on us the consideration how the capacity for doing good and better work can be developed and increased. The workers must be trained; and this is a necessity which grows upon us perceptibly with every decade. The broad question of general education, which of course has its due and direct relation to technical education, and to the efficiency of the worker, is happily taken up by the nation and made compulsory. We have abundant evidence of the value and importance of this in the fact that as education extends juvenile crime decreases, and with it the expenses of the police court; and what is still more cheering the homes of our poorer class of working people are by the direct influence of the children becoming more and more cheerful.

The other sphere of activity, in which the welfare of all business men is brought forward in discussion, and where necessary action taken, has been referred to in the chapter on the home-trade and kindred associations. Whether, therefore, the business man's life and action be considered from the commercial, the philanthropic, the moral, the educational, the industrial, or the social side, it is, if rightly regarded, a noble life, and in it may be developed the highest forces and capacities of a great mind. This may be said, of course, without depreciating in the slightest possible degree the grand callings of ministers of state and of professional men of every grade.

Many of the most capable men of business do yet another kind of service in undertaking the duties and responsibilities of municipal life, serving their fellow-citizens in the management of the affairs of the corporation. The importance of such services, gratuitously and often lavishly rendered, it would not be easy to over-estimate, the health and very much of the well-being of all the inhabitants of the town or city which they serve being the object of their labours. It is, perhaps, the culminating honour in the life of business men that their conduct, liberality, and intelligence should have so won the respect and confidence of a constituency as that they should be asked to be their representative in the national council at Westminster. But to him who has the fitness for the work and the time at his command it is only second to the parliamentary seat to have a place in the local parliament or council chamber. The duties of a town councillor are of such a character as to benefit the whole of the population within the range of the council's authority. To provide lighting, water, good and well-kept streets, a good sewage system, baths, public parks, and whatever else may minister to the health and happiness of the people, represents a large amount of labour and wise counsel. The first and important duty of the council is not, as some thoughtless people say, to levy rates and taxes; it is far higher, being no less than the devotion of the fruits of a vigorous life and ripened experience to the well-being of the people in the midst of whom life has been spent, and I don't hesitate to add that many members of our council bequeath to the City in value of labour and experience a sum equal to the gentleman who leaves his £10,000 or £20,000 to various charities, and are equally worthy of the esteem of their fellow citizens. As a rule our town councillors and aldermen are men who through life have satisfied the demand Cromwell made in lieu of his decayed serving men: "Give me men who make some conscience of what they do."

Turning to another aspect of the life of the business man, it will hardly be disputed that his surroundings and duties afford scope for the display and development of moral qualities in a very marked degree. He must for many a juncture and business crisis be a man of courage and resolution. There is often risk, sometimes adventure, and almost always enterprise to call his more daring aptitude into play. There is a constant making towards a goal, a fixed object of endeavour, in which he can find inspiration, and which kindles his enthusiasm. J. R. Lowell says of General McClellan that he had many excellent qualities, but he lacked enthusiasm. He had caution but no ardour. Caution in a business man is one of the most needful qualities, but no less in the warehouse than on the battle-field there is need for the head of a firm, of a department or of an office, to have the power of inspiring to effort those under his care and direction. He must feel and be able to make those about him feel that the business of his department and of the house he represents must be in the front rank by merit, giving his highest and best thought to making the opportunities which sometimes disappoint those who wait for them. Business men must be aggressive; they must be leaders, and not followers.

That enterprise may be and should be combined with caution, however, goes without saying. In business life, as in all other, discretion is the better part of valour; indeed, the courage of confidence and assurance can only be his who acts upon conviction and well-grounded expectancy. Such associations as the Manchester Trade Protection Society, and all other movements to secure a safe trade, only tend to foster the spirit of enterprise, and to distinguish it from risky speculation. The Trade Protection Society has for its membership a number of gentlemen representing the different branches of the trade of Manchester, who watch legislation in all matters affecting the trades of the district, taking action therein as circumstances seem to warrant.

The business world is ever testing the strength of the more personal moral qualities. No day passes without furnishing its opportunity of connivance with something wrong, until the principles of a man are fully understood and his integrity beyond attack. The man that connives at wrong will in his own character, and not unfrequently in his own circumstances, pay dearly for it. Reliability and trust are based upon integrity, and it is not difficult to see that the upright man stands in a position of command in the keen strife of the commercial life of to-day, the man whose "word is his bond." Scrupulous integrity is strength. "There is no mistake greater," says a writer, "than to suppose the conscience can do a little sin and not suffer; that little sin is the one weak point." It is the point of insecurity ever afterwards; it is the very prolific source of more sins.

It should be an axiom amongst all in positions of authority, that no man is fit to command who cannot command himself. Adam Smith says "self-command is not only in itself a great virtue, but from it all other virtues seem to derive their lustre." Retaliation often violates propriety, and leaves a twofold wrong in the place of one: the mistake or wrong of the offender, and the wrong done to oneself by hasty and ungoverned action. It is the vain and the weak man who has little self-control, and who thinks that a bullying manner shows spirit. "It should never be forgotten that we ought to show to those who happen to be placed within our power or who depend on us, forbearance, lenity, and reserve in using their services, and mildness in delivering commands. Each one should feel that he is forbidden to diminish the sum of human happiness, by enforcing unnecessary labour and confinement, or to insult his servants by harsh, scornful, or opprobrious language; nor ought harmless pleasures to be refused; and by the same principle of not diminishing the sum of human happiness, we are forbidden causeless or inconsiderate anger, habitual peevishness, and groundless suspicion." *

There is one other manly quality which business life is specially calculated to foster, and that is honourable emulation without envy or jealousy. Men who, by dint of hard work and continuous effort, have raised themselves to high positions in the world of commerce or in the firm to which they belong, are able to appreciate the like success in others, knowing its cost. Bitter feelings are sometimes engendered by a too-conscious rivalry; but the true state of mind and heart for a successful and happy business life is quite opposed both to such feelings and to any exhibition of them. There are many opportunities afforded of ruling down such unworthy impulses, and replacing them by manlier and more generous ones. Amidst all the discords and jealousies of this competitive age, when every man must sometimes feel impelled to join in Wordsworth's invocation to Milton—

>We are selfish men,
>Oh, raise us up, return to us again,
>And give us manners, virtue, freedom, powers,—

it is still possible to remain united and calm in the consciousness of power and rectitude; and the success which has placed others on a high pedestal will only evoke our esteem and minister to the spirit within us of true and noble emulation.

---

* Paley, in his chapter on Moral and Political Philosophy.

CHAPTER VII.
TO YOUNG MEN.

IN entering the business world, you are entering a school in which the lessons to be learnt are of the most broadening and absorbing character. Its teachings are on finance, law, politics (*i.e.*, the art of governing and administering), geography, specified industries, and, by no means least in importance, human nature. It is a school equally for moral training; men are born to greater aspirations and larger life by its discipline; they learn to bear and to forbear, to be patient under annoyance, to keep down wrath, to look mercifully on a poor, suffering, but honest debtor; to cheer the needy with timely encouragement and help, to inspire the desponding to effort. It is a capital school, if a man is true at heart, and has faith in himself and in a helping God.

Each new generation sees the intellectual life of the business world of a higher order. There is more to be learnt and known; new departments, new developments, new tastes bring with them not only more to be understood and grasped, but are ever introducing fresh problems for solution, the weighing of principle against principle and method against method, demanding the most careful and thoughtful attention. But when once this intelligent zeal is thrown into the various business operations of our city, there will be a restoration of the prestige which has for so many years attached to the name of the Manchester man of business.

A gentleman once remarked to the writer: "I don't see why a young fellow with means should put himself into a warehouse, and be shut up day by day dealing with a lot of nobodies, passing by opportunities for pleasure and intellectual culture in a better atmosphere and in better society." We grant it would not be difficult to find a more cheerful climate, and if a youth be fond of science, or study of any kind, he may do well by devoting himself to it; yet one would hardly say that the life of the commercial man, conducting a large home and shipping business, is such as to leave his mind uncultivated and unexpanded. He must be acquainted with the raw and manufactured products of almost every country, and must know the time to buy, and the requirements of his own customers in this and other countries before he enters upon his purchases. He has financial and banking arrangements with the various parts of the world to which he exports or from which he imports. He must be familiar with the rates of exchange, government regulations, and custom duties, and with modes of conveyance and freights. He must exercise constant supervision over the bleaching, dyeing, and finishing of goods. He must watch that the trade marks of his firm are not used by unscrupulous or innocent traders, be constantly in contact with men of real power, who have an intelligent grip of their business, and will have, in his capacity of trader, to deal with commodities in so many shapes and forms and in such varied operations. We say it is an honourable and useful life, however regarded; trade and commerce afford employment to the millions, revenue to the state, develop taste, extend and perfect civilisation, and give that knowledge of the world and of each other that the experience gained is of value in numerous ways amongst one's own countrymen or fellow-citizens.

Excellence is therefore worth attaining; aim at it. We shall never succeed in what we undertake unless we have high thoughts of its worth, and take pleasure in it. There is one practice or habit amongst youths and young men against which we would speak a word of warning. It is a common remark, and expresses a too common state of feeling: "I don't care; I do as much as my share," or "as much as I am paid for; and if my master will not allow me this or permit that, then I shall not do any more; I shall not trouble about saving him anything in any way." Now, nothing can be more contrary to your interest, from whatever point you view the matter. It is wrong in principle, and hazardous in practice. It is possible that your employer may be thoughtless and ungenerous, or that a fellow-servant may rise in favour by unfair means and beat you in the race; in either case nothing is gained by you by your assumption of carelessness. You are the loser in forfeiting the satisfaction and enjoyment of having done your duty, of having used every faculty and power you possess in your work. The evidence of a thousand records and the experience of thousands more point to the reward, and prove it to be as certain as anything human that toil and patience will win at last. The old saying is a good one, " Two blacks do not make a white "—they are but two blacks in the end. As a point of honour, as a point of prudence, regard your duty as sacred; discharge to the full extent of your mental and physical powers the work that you have undertaken; it is worth doing well; excellence is worth attaining; and no one ought to expect to reap where he has not sown. In speaking of success and aiming at it, it is well to remember the truth illustrated by Emerson in his *Conduct of Life*, that "Concentration may be made very greatly the source of energy with many. Concentration stops all miscellaneous activity, and directs our force on one or a few points, as the gardener, by severe pruning, forces the sap of the tree into one or two vigorous limbs, instead of suffering it to spindle into a sheaf of twigs . . . the one prudence, therefore, in life is concentration; the one evil, dissipation."

To win success in business, as in everything else, you must be strong as men. The *man* is the *thinker*. Our power to think is our power to know, and "knowledge is power." We must bend to the laws that environ us. Bend to Nature's laws, and she will rejoice your heart; bend to moral laws, and your reward will be greater still. The price must be paid for strength of life and success in it. "Grudge not labour, grudge not pain, sorrow, disappointment, or distress of any kind;—all is for your good if you can endeavour and endure." Better counsel was never given than this of Carlyle's to a young aspirant to literary fame. If success is to be ours, we must win it, and often wrest it from adverse circumstance. The truest life is that which is itself a growth; which grows by pain and learns from disappointment to endeavour and endure. Nothing can be said of a man more hopeful and inspiring than that he is growing; nothing more dispiriting and hopeless than that he has ceased to grow. Whatever our business circumstance, we should see to it that we are growing as men; there is eternal promise in that, and we shall be ready, fortified in spirit and in wisdom, to seize the golden opportunity when it presents itself. There can be no more doubtful commendation of a man than to say he is contented. Rest and content are not for man. Restlessness, *i.e.*, with regard to ourselves and our progress, is divine evidence that we are born for immortality. A growing manhood is not attained by merely furnishing a favourable environment; surroundings minister to it; but the birth and growth of a higher manhood of courage, rectitude, and love, go on within the man. Grow yourself, and your circumstances will grow with you; if they do not, *you* are not the less; if your circumstances grow and you do not, you will present an anomaly comparable to the state of manhood's " sixth age," whose " hose " are " a world too wide for his shrunk shank."

All men need recreation, but none so much as youths and young men; your physical frame and mental powers are growing, and both must have exercise for their healthy development. If your work is manual, you need mental recreation; if your work is mental, you need physical recreation. Manly pastimes are to be found of both kinds. Amongst the former are chess and some games with cards; amongst the latter, such outdoor sports as cricket, football, lacrosse, cycling, and the gymnasium. Early manhood requires the moral aid of absorbing pastimes, especially such as give vent to the animal spirits of youth, and help to subdue its passions.

Let us put to you concisely and frankly what we desire to advise :—

I. Young men should find one or more smart, manly young fellows with whom to associate for purposes of society and recreation. Above all, be judicious in your choice of a girl companion; a good wife is the highest prize a man can win; but do not be led away by the fascinations of a dressy, giddy girl, who has no backbone of character. Such a one will soon cease to be a companion; you would then crave and seek other society; habits of drinking and gambling and worse often ensue; and we have seen again and again manly and honourable young men fall step by step, until at last they stand before the magistrate for disorderly conduct or neglect of home. Noble friendships strengthen the heart in virtue, *i.e.*, in valour or manliness: evil friendships corrupt the soul.

II. Find time to read useful and good books; make companions of them. They will be an unfailing source of strength to you in any position of life you may be called to occupy.

III. Be scrupulous in all points of honour. Never do a girl a wrong, nor trifle with her affections; be true and loyal in friendship; honourable in all your service, industrious and truthful. In business, be accurate in your statements, do not exaggerate with regard to anything you may have to sell. We have always said that a man who tells a lie is wanting in brain power; if he cannot conduct a case in court, transact business in the office, or sell goods at the counter without telling falsehoods, he is not possessed of the qualifications needful for the position he holds; there should be no dallying with the question of truth. To resort to falsehood is to make a confession of weakness. Take the case of a young man of moderately good education, who does not read a good solid book in twelve months, and who consequently is doing little to mature his mind, widen his judgment, and increase his knowledge of men and things. He is placed by the side of a well-educated young fellow who is constantly developing his intellectual powers. The latter carries through his work with success and confidence; the former, however, is conscious of comparative failure; he is anxious to be the equal of the man of trained mind, and resorts to lying and deceit, making the excuse that he is driven to it in order to do his trade and maintain his position. The fact is, and it is a fact which will sooner or later be made manifest, that he is wanting in capacity or administrative ability, and he is left behind in the race not only by the man who, like himself, had the advantage of education, but by the man who has not many words in his vocabulary, and who is painfully conscious of the want of early education, yet who is so sterling in character and so reliable in every way that he commands the admiration of his customers and of his employers and wins for himself a good position. Of course, where education and ability are combined with integrity, the man possessing all these qualities rises to the highest position; but it is wisdom for every man, whatever his capabilities and advantages, to be strictly truthful and honest, remembering that honesty includes punctuality, faithful service, and the use only of one's own and not of another man's goods or time, and that truthfulness means saying what is strictly correct, and in the clearest language you can command. The advice said to have been given by an Oldham man to a friend will bear repetition: "I have tried both sorts, but I have found out that honesty is the best policy."

IV. Do not be carried away by false ambition. There is a weak ambition, founded on conceit, which greatly ensnares some young men. Many are exceedingly anxious to be thought something they are not; they ape their superiors in habit and style of living. From our own observation and frequent conversations with men of experience, we have learned that disaster often arises from this source. A young man gets into a warehouse or office, and, after being there a few years, is receiving a salary of, say, £120 per annum. He is acquainted with another young man in the same house, perhaps a year or two his junior, receiving, it may be, £150 per annum. He feels himself quite the latter's equal, possibly is so, and could have filled the better position quite as ably if it had been his good fortune to secure it. He is quite as popular in the club, in the cricket or football field, and he is desirous to appear just as well as the other; so he must pay to this and subscribe to that, live in as good apartments, smoke the same cigars, undergoing all the expenses with his income of £120 which cost the other nearly the whole of his £150. Instead of studying the rule of three to find out what must be the result, he only studies the rule of two, viz., his wants and the source from which they are to be supplied. He is not long before he finds a source of supply in trifling thefts. His master will not voluntarily give him more money; he cannot borrow, and we believe it is often under a sense of disappointment, and the feeling that he has a right to a larger remuneration, that the first robberies are committed. He grows in boldness as he remains for a time undiscovered, only to wake up to the discovery that there is a rule of three, the third factor being the apportionment of justice by the magistrate. Have patience and wait. Keep company with young men of intelligence and character, whose pleasure is in reasonable and inexpensive recreation. By all means seek recreation; take part in athletic games, which will help to make better men of you in every sense; but live within your position and means. Don't ape the great, but aim at it; and if you have brain-power, tact, and energy, you will reach your goal. It would be well if every young man in this city would honestly consider his position. If you are the son of a merchant or professional man, and have the capacity of your father, do you labour as he laboured? Do you give the time and attention, and bestow the amount of thought upon your calling that he has done? If so your future is secure. But if you have less ability, are morose, wanting in urbanity, are given to tall talk, and give three or four hours a day to your duties where your father gave ten, then the result will be the want of success, which it is fair and just to expect. There are always about you industrious, aspiring young men, fired by a worthy ambition to excel, who are capable of stepping into your place. You have the start of them, and if you avail yourselves of it, you will retain the lead and win the regard of all ; but if you throw the position away, do not blame your successor, the fault is your own.

The only safe course is to accept cheerfully your present position, and determine that you will only move out of it by dint of industry and application. Happiness is the lot of the man who lives within his income and manfully accepts his position in life, seeking to improve himself that he may be ready for the day of greater things. There are thousands of men in this city earning from twenty-five to fifty shillings a week, who have more real domestic and personal enjoyment, who are more respected and have a higher reputation amongst their equals and amongst men in higher stations than themselves, than the thousands who receive larger incomes and make the spendthrift's use of them. We do not say, of course, that poverty is a blessing, but integrity and moderation are. He has not touched the first rung of the ladder which leads to an honourable position and to a strong and manly life, who speaks to his fellow-salesman or clerk as a member of the goody-goody class because he prefers to go to a lecture or to classwork, instead of to the club to play billiards or to the theatre or hotel for the evening.

V. There is a pride which is a serious hindrance to many youths. Fresh from successes at school or indulgence at home, they think their capacity is considerably above the average, and that they should not be called upon to do any work that seems drudgery to them. Now, this drudgery is part of the training for business life, and an essential part. Nobody can fill the higher positions well who has not learned to fill the lower. He cannot understand with the same clearness how the work of the subordinates should be done, nor can he confer on them the benefit of raising them to great proficiency.

The same kind of pride impels some to seek positions for which they are totally unqualified. One would not stifle any true, energetic purpose; but many young men do seriously miss their calling, and fall into grievous trouble, in which unfortunately others are involved. It is a mark of instability and must end in ruinous consequences for a youth to decline to take the advice of those who have experienced the arduousness of life, and seen the inevitable fate of vain, incompetent men.

A true magnanimity can only grow up in the modest, self-contained man. To over-rate one's self and under-rate one's fellow-worker greatly mars a life, and it is a source of blindness as to elements of weakness in one's self and strength in others. The failure to see another's merit is blindness to merit; failure to recognise one's own defects is one of its most baneful results.

VI. Allow us now to indicate one or two of the dangers which arise from the temptations besetting the lives of the young men of to-day. We refer to smoking, drinking, and gambling. All young people should abstain from intoxicating drinks and from tobacco, at least until they are matured both in physical powers and in judgment—say, until they are twenty-three or twenty-four; after that period everyone should be able to exercise restraint over himself, and probably will be able if untainted by early habit. We have not the slightest desire to dictate, being in no sense a fanatic, and having no wish to curtail young men's legitimate pleasures; but to our certain knowledge many young men indulge in these habits who cannot afford to do so, and who have to deny themselves the means of education, decent clothing, and in some cases even proper food. These habits often lead on to other modes of expenditure quite inimical to their interests, and many have confessed to us that they have started on a downward path by smoking and just taking a glass with a friend. Again and again we pass in the streets the wrecks of once respectable young people whom we have known in business.

The following figures are very striking, showing the number of years men of given ages are expected to live according as they are temperate or intemperate:—

Years of age.	Temperate.	Intemperate.
20	44	15
30	36	13
40	28	11
50	21	10
60	14	6

A question on which we feel very strongly is that of gambling and its increasing prevalence. Again, the writer would say, in order that he be not misunderstood, that he believes in the necessity for amusement and exercise as a means of recreation for young people. It has come under our observation for some years that a good athlete generally turns out a good man in whatever calling; and one of our medical men once said, " Let us see what sort of hips and thighs a lad has, never mind his head; I want to see physical power." It is no less true that the young of both sexes need games for their employment during winter evenings; some prefer billiards, others chess, others dice, dominoes, draughts, or cards. One can have no objection to these as games, but there is much that is to be condemned in playing for money. Why the first question, when a game is decided upon, should be, " What shall we play for ?" and why the remark should be so often heard, " I cannot play well unless I have something at stake," we cannot understand. It is simply a habit, and one that often leads to great mischief. We regard gambling in every form as unmanly, unreasonable, and ungodly. We regard gambling as unmanly, because it is necessarily enfeebling in its effects upon the will. "The man who 'has a bet on' is, in many cases, a purely passive spectator of the rise and fall of his fortunes, so soon as ever his bet is made. Unless he descend to dishonourable practices—a possibility too mean to be now entered into—he has nothing to do but to await the issue and accept it. Nothing can be more enfeebling to the will than this self-imposed passivity. The man is teaching himself to depend on luck, whereas the active pursuit of ends, whether by plodding or pushing, is the mark of the energetic will. A strong man always has a strong hand in the determining of his own fortunes. A distinction holds in some sense between games of skill for chance and mere speculation, but in so far as gambling leads men away from the paths of labour which support themselves, minister to their strength of character and serve others, the practice is unmanly."

Mr. S. Laing, in his work on *Modern Science and Thought*, says: "Perhaps the commonest of all delusions is that of being born under a lucky star. A man gambles, bets, or speculates because he thinks he is lucky and sure to win. Now, there is in reality no such thing as luck; it is all a question of averages. The only approach to what may be called luck is that a fool will probably have more of it than a wise man, for as the fool foresees nothing, whenever fortune's die turns up in his favour, he sets it down to luck; while the wise man, who has schemed and worked for the event, calls it foresight. But the actual average of events which depend entirely on chance will be the same.

"If a man plays at *rouge et noir*, with one chance in a hundred in favour of the bank, it is certain that if he plays often enough he will lose his capital once at least for every hundred times he plays; or if he speculates on the Stock Exchange, the turn of the market and brokers' commission will in the long run certainly swallow up his original capital. And yet men will gamble and speculate because they cannot resist the pleasing illusion that they are lucky, and that it would be very nice to win a large stake without having had to work for it."

Betting on horses is the most serious form of gambling that comes under our observation. We have seen and heard so much of this practice and its effects, that our horror of it exceeds anything that we can express in words. If we could reach the eye, or ear, or the understanding of the young men of this city, we would earnestly appeal to them to avoid it; the way of the gambler is bestrewed with sorrow and anxiety, and generally ends in great distress to himself and family. We could give numerous instances of a most painful character where young men, feeling themselves bound by this so-called " debt of honour," have robbed their employers, lost character and situation, and blasted the proud hopes of good parents. We know there are some men who indulge in the practice in a small and comparatively innocent form and get no particular harm, but these are the exceptions; and the great fact holds that we have no right to get another person's money without giving that *quid pro quo* in some shape, and the cultivation of the habit leads in numberless cases to ruin. This in itself proves the unreasonableness of the practice; but the very basis of gambling, and especially of betting, is an irrational one, and this because a profit is made, when it is made, not out of knowledge but out of ignorance. In all rational pursuit of wealth the chances for all increase as the knowledge of all widens. Though the capitalist and labouring classes are often regarded and spoken of as competing the one against the other for their share of the produce of industry, it is none the less true that each is richer by the other's knowledge. The wider the information of the master, the keener his foresight, and the surer his grasp of manufacturing and commercial principles, the better captained and the better paid his men. The more thorough the education, both general and technical, and the greater the knowledge and mental powers of the employé, the higher is his value to his master. In every rational and healthy pursuit of wealth, the knowledge of one becomes the benefit of all. In gambling, the reverse is the case. Ignorance is capitalised. What the bookmaker or private betting man depends upon is not the knowledge, but the ignorance of his client or victim, as one may prefer to call him. Of course, there are two parties to a bet, each willingly entering into it; and the same is true of either party, each is hoping to profit by the other's ignorance. The fact that most bets take the form of "odds against," offered and taken, shows that a certain quantity of ignorance in one mind is pitted against an equal, less a greater quantity of ignorance in another mind. Ben Brierley, writing in the *Manchester Guardian* upon "gradely folk," gives a definition of "lump-yeads." This "term," he says, "was wont to be applied to young bar-parlour men who read nothing but sporting papers, who pretended to know everything, but knew nothing except how to silence modest intelligence by the offer of a bet." The term "lump-yead," coupled with the definition of it, shows that Ben Brierley regards the practice as irrational.

Certainly the practice is ungodly, for it is intensely selfish. The winner only profits by another's loss. If life seems slow, look around you, and, in addition to many healthy modes of physical enjoyment, you will find opportunity for the exercise of your mental powers, and perchance in some such noble form as the help of your fellows, instead of ministering to their ruin. Learn, at least, to possess yourselves in patience. Do not seek another's wealth. Toil manfully for your living, and endeavour to improve your circumstances. Hold yourselves independent of pity, by being men of will and not creatures of chance. Command respect by the creation of wealth rather than the wresting it from another.

We only speak of young men's dangers in order, if possible, to awaken your desires for a true and worthy life. We would create an enthusiasm for great and good things. Each man that is true in all his dealings, magnanimous and unselfish, is a power for good amongst his fellows. "A man," said Isaiah, "shall be as the shadow of a great rock in a weary land." And any man who yields to the better impulses within him may live nobly, doing his part in the world's uplifting.

> No life
> Can be pure in its purpose and strong in its strife,
> And all life not be purer and stronger thereby.

Some time ago a gentleman called at a large house in this city, asking if he could be supplied with goods and could have credit for a certain amount, on the usual trade terms, stating he was in business in such a city, in a country far away across the waters which it takes weeks to reach. Questions were put to him as to his family connections, early training and experience, financial position, and the reasons why he had left his native land and adopted the place in which he now resides. He replied, "This is rather a new experience you are putting me through, but it will afford me pleasure to answer all your enquiries, and I will give you a short narrative of my life, especially that part of it which has been spent abroad. Not succeeding in this country as one would desire, the ground being too well covered and occupied by intelligent, pushing young men, who were like myself, anxious to make a position. I had served my time to the dry goods trade, and felt competent to take a responsible situation. Finding the way difficult here, I resolved to try my fortune on another shore. After casting about and making enquiries I decided that the country where my business is now conducted was, on the whole, the best I could select. I bade adieu to my family and friends and crossed the ocean, landing at a large seaport town. Was in good health, had a little money in my pocket, possessing fair average abilities for the business in which I had so far been engaged, called upon the various wholesale and retail dealers, offering my services at a moderate salary. Weeks passed by and no probability appeared of finding occupation; whatever report was given of my experience, however low the salary offered to be accepted, all seemed in vain. My patience was severely tried; my funds were getting smaller, but I was determined not to return home. I started out one morning resolute upon finding something, even if it was carrying coals or wheeling a barrow. I had not been out long before a paper in a window caught my eyes, on which was written 'A bottler wanted.'

Entering the office I asked what kind of work a bottler had to perform. The reply was prompt and decisive, 'Bottling ale.' 'Can I see the work, sir?' Reply: 'Yes, if you open the door before you.' Opening the door, saw a number of men and youths all vigorously engaged bottling ale. Then immediately returned to the office, and said to the gentleman 'I have seen the work. What are the wages?' He replied, 'Twenty-four shillings per week.' I expressed my willingness to accept the situation, feeling sure I could do it well, after a day's practice. An engagement was made, and for some months I diligently followed my new occupation. One day a junior was larking, and threw a half-pint bottle at another youth. It missed him and passed through the window. It was soon arranged that the square must be replaced. A plumber was sent for, and I watched the operation of taking out the remaining part of the old glass and the putting in of the new square. When it was done, enquired of the man what he would charge. He named the price, and I then asked what was the cost of the diamond with which he cut the glass. He told me, and also the cost of the glass and putty. The profit seemed to me very large. It was quite clear, if a fair amount of work could be found it was a vastly better-paying business than bottling ale. Having thought this over a few days, I called upon a large plumber and got all particulars as to the cost of the glass, putty, diamond, &c., which would be required to start a man in a small way. After a good many experiments, became confident I could do the work satisfactorily, and having money enough in my possession to enable me to make the start, I left my situation, determining to leave the coast and work up country, calling upon shopkeepers, at private houses, and farmhouses, putting in squares, where they had broken ones, at a moderate price. My stock was soon used up, and had to be replenished on a rather larger scale. This was repeated again and again, until I found myself a little better off. Then I thought if I could find a decent town where there was room for a new trader, it would be well to see if I could not make a start in business premises of my own instead of tramping the country. Shortly after that I met with a place which seemed everything I could desire. Returned to the city, stated to a large wholesale store what I had seen, named the extent of my capital, and asked if they would supply me with sufficient goods to open the store, on which they could have any security they liked, and I would see them with full particulars at fixed times, and feeling sure they would find me a good customer. The proposal was considered. In due time I was allowed to select the necessary stock, and I returned to my new home, which was to be my centre of action for the future. Then I opened the store, and succeeded in winning the confidence of the people in and around the town. I gradually extended the size of the store, increased the quantity and variety of goods, and now I am free from all liability; have a large, general stock; and (taking a book out of his breast pocket) now have that amount to my credit, in my bankers' hands, viz., £10,000, which I should like you to get confirmed by writing to my bankers, or their agents in London." The statement as to capital and character was fully endorsed. To the mind of the present writer this is an interesting record of what can be accomplished by a man who is resolute in working his own way and fighting his own battle in life.

Chapter VIII.

RECOLLECTIONS OF MR. JOHN WADE.

AMONGST the many remarkable men we have met, during our sojourn in this city, was a Mr. Wade. His first entry into Manchester was made as a drover, bringing a number of cattle from Yorkshire to a butcher in this city. Something in his manner arrested the attention of the butcher, who said to him, as he was about to return, "Young man, have you engaged to go back immediately?" "No, sir, I am in no hurry," was the reply. "Well, then, stop here a few days; I am in need of a helper, and have work to do for which I think you are well fitted."

He remained, and did his work so well that at the close of the first week his master said to him, "I see you will suit me, and should like you to stay awhile. I will give you so much wages." The offer was accepted and the work entered upon at once. During the first week, the master spoke to his new employé about his interest as a sabbath school scholar, and said, "I see you are a steady young man, and I should like you to go to the chapel we attend and also to the Sunday school, in which my daughter and I take a deep interest."

John Wade replied, "I am sorry to say I can neither read nor write."

"Never mind, you can go to the young men's class, and you will find the teacher a very kind and agreeable man."

He consented; but on entering the school the superintendent, seeing he was a fine, manly fellow (he stood five feet ten or eleven inches, and was well built), at once asked him to take charge of a class of which the teacher was unavoidably absent that afternoon. This was more that the young man had expected.

"Oh," said he, "you must excuse me, I am not used to teaching."

"Never mind, you will easily manage a lot of nice little fellows like these."

The young man was too proud to expose his ignorance, and determined to try and do his best. He would watch the next teacher's movements, and, as far as possible, would copy them; besides, he remembered that his master had explained to him how the class in which he was to have been placed was conducted, so he sat down among the boys. One of the lads remarked, "Our teacher is going through the gospel of St. John, and we are at such a chapter;" and they all turned at once to the place. Meantime, John had opened his testament, but unfortunately at the wrong part, which the nearest lad saw in a moment, and called attention to the fact. "Yes, yes," he said, "you are younger than I, I will take your book." The exchange was made, and they began to read. The third boy stumbled at a word and looked to the teacher for assistance. Without exhibiting for a moment his incapacity, he at once realised his position, and turning to the fourth boy said, in a cheerful voice, "Now, my lad, always be ready to help your neighbour." By adopting this plan the whole of the chapter was safely got through, but not in much comfort on John's part. Every moment he had been growing warmer, a fact which became plainly visible in his face; his discomfort being, no doubt, intensified by the unusual confinement in a well-filled room, and by his attire, so very different from that to which he was accustomed. Part of this had been provided for him from his master's wardrobe, and part bought at a second-hand clothes shop. In spite of his misery, however, John tried to follow the example of the teachers round him, and talked to the boys until the bell rang and teaching ceased. An address was then delivered, after which the school closed, very much to the joy of the new teacher, who had more than once promised himself, "no one should catch him there again."

Being questioned on his return as to his success, he told them his experience, and the torture he had gone through, adding, "I shall never be caught in that position again; I will go to the chapel, but no more school for me, thank you; at any rate, not at present." "Oh, don't say so," returned the master. "I will tell you what we can do. We shall know the chapter to be read in the young men's class, and we will read it over every morning and night this week; when I cannot afford the time, my daughter shall read it with you, and explain as much as possible. In a week you will have nearly learned it by heart, and know it quite well enough, at any rate, to take your place in the class. Do, I beg, go again; if not in a week, say, in a fortnight." The latter was promised, the effort was made, and he acquired sufficient confidence to continue. The reading and explanation at home went on for some time, the progress being so marked that he was soon able to render considerable help, both at the chapel and as a teacher in the school, to both of which he gave generously out of his earnings. Meantime, his manifest business ability had secured the warmest approval of the master and his wife. It was soon discovered by the former that the teaching and reading of his daughter were more appreciated than his own, and that she, on her part, never found the time devoted to it too long or the task inconvenient, but was always ready each evening to give the required assistance. So one day John called his employer aside, and said that " his daughter Sarah had not only been very successful in giving him lessons for the school, but had also, at the same time, won his affections, and they had mutually agreed that, with her father and mother's approval, they should be married." After due consideration, the consent was given, and the two were very soon united. They had not been married long before John saw that his father-in-law was in difficulties. He could not, as in days gone by, go into the market, and buy, paying ready money for his cattle. Being questioned on the matter, he disclosed to his son-in-law the fact of his insolvency. John replied, "Don't say a word to anyone. I have saved £120 since entering your service, and that, it properly managed, will be quite sufficient to restore your position in the market. I will take charge of the business, only give me your confidence, let me take my own way, and we will soon put all right again." This was agreed upon, and then John, whom in future we must call Mr. Wade, went to his wife, told her what had passed, and said, "Now, we must for a few years exercise the strictest economy. What do you think we can manage the house upon, to cover all expenses, except rent and rates?" She thought the matter over carefully and named an amount. "Very well," he said, "you shall have that sum weekly." Mr. Wade continued perseveringly and energetically to push the business, which increased every year, and the father lived to see and enjoy not only the old position of financial ease and comfort, but to see his son-in-law accumulating a fortune. During these few years, the thrifty young wife, who had all along silently borne the grief, which a true child was sure to feel at the reverse of fortune which had overtaken her parents, had been saving every shilling she could, until she had accumulated £120. One morning she came into the sitting-room, saying, "John, see!" at the same time pouring out of a bag £120 in gold, with the remark, "I have saved this out of the money you have given me for housekeeping; this pays my father's debt, does it not?" He looked at her, but his heart was too full to speak. Years after, when he was advanced in life, the strong man wept as he related this to me. On Sunday, he and his wife and servant always went to chapel, locking up the house. Having money always on the premises, he felt it was his duty to give any person, who might break in, as much trouble as possible to find it. Therefore, every Saturday night, he put the notes and loose cash in a bag, one week placing this under a mattress, the next in a wardrobe, so varying its hiding-place every time. On one occasion he thought he would conceal it under the fireplace, as far back as possible. It so happened, that particular evening, there was an extra service at chapel, to which Mr. and Mrs. Wade remained, the latter telling the servant to go home and light a fire in the sitting-room, as it was rather cold. She did so. On their return, Mr. Wade at once caught sight of the fire, and, remembering the money, he rushed to the grate, and dragged from beneath the still unburnt bag, all safe. Shortly after this, to his great sorrow, his beloved wife was prostrated by a severe and fatal illness. After her death he retired from business, investing his capital in various ways, including house and shop property. He made his will, appointing several well-known gentlemen in the city as executors, and, having no children of his own, left his property, which was very considerable, to various charities and educational institutions. Shortly after he sent for me, and expressed his extreme annoyance at the treatment he had received from a gentleman connected with one of these institutions, who ought not to have been guilty of such indiscretions as were repeated to me. The result was, the first will was destroyed, and another made, leaving the property to a large number of nephews and nieces, many of whom he had never seen.

Though uncultured, not having had the blessing of a good education and training, such as many have, he was, nevertheless, as fine in spirit and purpose as in personal appearance, and though in common with all human beings he had faults, he had many high qualities. He was keen, shrewd, and far-seeing, yet at the same time generous and helpful to many. Mr. Wade had one peculiarity, he would never have recourse to legal measures; if his debtors would not pay without the intervention of the law, the accounts remained unpaid. From the day he entered Manchester, without a decent coat or pair of shoes, to the time of his death, when he was in comparatively affluent circumstances, we never heard of his owing any man a debt. He would keep no books, his business was a cash one, and whatever advantages could be secured by cash payments he was always prepared to take. His career was in many respects a pattern. Would that we had more young men like him! Where now are those who would be found willing to endure the ordeal he passed through in his early Sunday school labours? He was a hero in his position, putting pride completely aside, when by so doing he could secure the improvement of his mind and the good of others. One cannot but admire his action, when his father-in-law's position became known to him, in laying down his hard-earned money, and resolutely determining by his own efforts to maintain the family honour, and return in no stinted form the kindness the old gentleman had shown him, when he was a poor and comparatively destitute lad; nay, the very opportunity, as he told me, gave him great delight. We would not conclude without one further word of praise for his thrifty wife, who with pardonable pride desired to save her father's good name by paying his debt out of her own careful savings, the result of frugal management.

Chapter IX.

ADDRESSES.

RAILWAYS A CIVILISING FORCE.

I WOULD remind you that you are living in a town which is now widely known. The rapid growth of the population of Crewe during the last twenty or thirty years has been remarkable, and it was only in just recognition of its position amongst the thriving and populous towns of the country that it was placed on the list of municipal boroughs. The way in which the members of the corporation had discharged the important and responsible duties of their position had shown the wisdom of this arrangement, and had resulted in a new and improved state of things in the borough. We are favoured this evening with the presence of your chief magistrate, and you will, I am sure, join with me in giving him a hearty welcome. The great railway company which gives employment to so large a portion of the population of Crewe is deserving of our highest appreciation; but we must not forget the other firms and companies who, seeing the character of the Crewe people, and knowing that there was a large number of unemployed females, had come and established places of business in their midst, finding occupation for those who would otherwise have led comparatively useless lives, and in many cases have been a burden to their parents and families. It is also pleasing to hear from those amongst you who are capable of forming an accurate judgment that, apart from trade and its immediate surroundings, there are many signs of progress to be found in your institutions, both literary, scientific, and political, and, I may add, religious also. This development will, I hope, be more manifest as years roll on; and I trust that you will rise still higher in the social scale, and become a centre of light and power in the county of Chester. You will pardon me now if, for a short time, I refer to a matter which affects the trades, both wholesale and retail, of all towns, namely, the carriage of parcels by post and by passenger trains. Your worthy mayor will at once see the importance of the effort we are making to secure a postal service to all parts of the empire, taking parcels up to four pounds weight for a small charge. Some say we should press for seven pounds, but at present we are aiming at four pounds only; and if this is secured it will be found an immense boon to all parties. Then we shall go to the railway companies and ask them to grant a concession, and allow parcels up to twenty-eight pounds to be sent by passenger trains at a low charge, according to distance. From careful inquiry, we feel convinced that the result will be a great advantage to the railways, and a great help to traders throughout the kingdom. We appeal to the railway companies to meet this just and business-like request. We must remember that railways are in a sense a monopoly. They are not simply to be looked upon as dividend-making institutions. They are great factors in the development of our national life. They are essential to our position if we are to maintain our commercial standing. Nay, more, the supplying of the very needs of the people, socially and mentally, depends largely upon them. The changes which the introduction of the railway system has wrought in this country cannot be stated or estimated. The current of thought is changed, the habits and customs of the people are improved, the style of dress, aye, and even the very language of our rural population have been materially altered. Now-a-days you do not ask men *how* they can move this or that weight of material; but what it will cost, and which is the best company to send it by. You do not ask the distance from town to town; but how long will it take by such a train. We do not discuss about the time *when* we shall be able to see such and such a book or paper; but it is ordered to be here or there in the morning. The railways are in this and also in other ways a great civilising force. They have done in large measure in India what all the talking of sages and good men could not have effected in a century, they have helped to break down caste. Men of different castes, who used to walk apart from each other, as far apart as the width of the street, and would not meet in any room, now rub together as they get their railway tickets, and, to save the difference between first and third class fares, will all ride together third class. They have found out that it makes no difference to them morally or physically; that they are just the same whether they touch each other or not; and so, in a while, it is to be hoped that they will, by receiving further light, discover that they have one common father and one common home above. Much more might be said if time would permit, but I will not detain you further. The railways should be deemed to be on a higher platform than ordinary business ventures; the public wants should be consulted, every convenience consistent with justice and reason should be afforded, and the request now put forward is certainly within their power to grant; and the granting the same would add one more to the many wise and prudent changes that have been made for the general good.

Chapter X.

NANTWICH AND ITS BATHS.

My friends,—In the name of Messrs. Rylands' firm, I have again the pleasure of wishing you a happy new year. Another point in our history has been reached, and if we look back upon the year past it must be to find out the weak points and see how and where we can improve them. At the commencement of the year many promises were made and many hopes cherished, and we confess some of them have not been realised; still if we were individually brought to the test, though we should speak of some dark days, we should also remember we have had "joys." If there have been fierce fightings, there has also been a season of peace and rest; and as we turn our faces now to the future, let it be with good heart. Let us play the man, and go on in hope and confidence. I have twice had the pleasure of visiting your neighbouring town of Nantwich, on the last occasion in company with a gentleman who, like myself, had a desire to know more of the town and district, and also to ascertain, if possible by personal experience, the effects of the brine baths, about which we had heard and read much. Before referring more definitely to the baths, allow me to say a few words about the town. Nantwich has a population of about seven thousand, and is situated on the banks of the Weaver, four miles from Crewe, on the Shrewsbury line of the London and North-Western Railway. It is the centre of an interesting group of fine old family mansions occupied by persons of distinction. These are Crewe Hall, Beeston Castle, Peckforton Castle, and Combermere Abbey. The latter has become famous in recent years by its having been made the residence during the hunting season of the Empress of Austria. Leland says: "In the reign of Henry VIII. there were three hundred salt mines open in Nantwich, but in the early part of the seventeenth century they were greatly reduced in number. Other and superior pits were opened in the vale of the Weaver, and having the advantage of water carriage, caused a continuous decline of the Nantwich pits, and ultimately they were abandoned." In reading the history of Cheshire, I was much surprised to find that in the reign of Henry I., in 1113, the town was laid waste by the Welsh; and again, in 1282, King Edward had necessity laid upon him to protect the corn and provisions of the inhabitants against a further approach of the Welsh army. In 1438 the town was consumed by fire, and again in 1583. On the 10th December it chanced, as it is expressed in the parish register, "that a most terrible and vehement fyre, beginning at the Water Lode about six of the clock at night, in a kitchen by brewing, the wynde being very boysterouse increased the said fyre, which verie vehementlie burned and consumed in the space of 15 hours six hundred bayes of buildings, and could not be stayed neither by laboure nor pollice, which I thought good to commend to posterity as a favourable punishment of the Almightie in destroying the buildings and goods onlie; by God's mercie but onlie two persons perished by fyre." In the year 1585 another entry was made in the parish register, which runs thus: "This year passed youre most noble Queen Elizabeth (whom God long preserve), of her royal and princelie bountie, granted a commission under her own hand to make a general collection throughout all the realm of England for the re-edyfying of this town of Nantwich, which liberalitie was collected in the year aforesaid, and this year followinge, the Queen contributing £2,000 herself, together with the necessary timber from the Delamere forests, and a number of the houses then erected remain to this day." I wonder whether anyone in the year 2184, speaking about Crewe and its past history, will be able to point to houses erected at this date—1885—as still existing. I trow not. In 1587 the town was visited with a kind of "frenzie or mad ague." The old town seems to have had a series of troubles in the shape of plague, fire, and pestilence, but it survived them all. At one time it was an important garrison, and was always loyal and firm in its devotion to Parliament. There are a number of interesting old buildings which I cannot stay now to describe, but I must make reference to the grand old church. It is a structure in the Gothic-Decorated style of architecture, with a fine octagonal tower rising from the centre. Passing some good business premises, which would do credit to many principal streets in our large towns, we came to High Street, and at the lower and extreme end adjoining the river we found the Town Hall—a large and somewhat handsome building, at the back of which the brine baths are situated. Going through the hall, which seems to be used for a variety of purposes, we entered the bath buildings. The town, as I have already stated, is pleasantly situated, surrounded by many places of interest easily reached on foot by pedestrians or visited in short drives, and would, therefore, to our minds, warrant an effort being made to accommodate individuals or families wishing for temporary residences to secure the benefit of the baths. The building known as the town hall could be adapted to the purpose with a moderate outlay, and if I may be pardoned for making a suggestion, it would be that the company should enlarge with the understanding that after all proper expenses are paid and five per cent. per annum given to the shareholders, the residue, if any, should be handed over, under the direction of the shareholders through the board of directors, to the various charities of the town such as now exist or may hereafter be established for the education and the moral and social improvement of the people. Of course, I am assuming it would be a fully-licensed hotel, but it being no profit to the proprietors to push the sale of wine and spirits, I apprehend they would be little used. As to the effect of the brine baths I cannot speak from personal experience, but if I may express an opinion formed upon what I have read of the Nantwich, Droitwich, and other brine baths, their curative qualities must be very unmistakeable. One of our medical gentlemen says we have only to turn over the leaves in the book of nature, and there we shall find a remedy for every ailment, an antidote for every poison. The time, he says, is fast approaching when the use of drugs will almost die away, and the various medicine given for different diseases will be to a great extent supplanted by the use of brine baths, diet, and hygiene. These baths, they say, will cure almost all diseases to which poor humanity is liable. In his extreme anxiety to enforce this fact, one doctor in a pamphlet which I read cries out in a sort of agony, "Oh, that the muse of some departed orator would inspire my pen so that the emphasis I lay upon the great value of Nantwich brine might be accepted"; and then he goes on to say in reference to cholera, the frightful disease which has been so devastating the Continent during the year just closed, "When I have tried almost every medicine and failed, so surely do tepid brine baths act as an almost certain cure." It was the extraordinary cures effected by taking several cholera cases to the saltworks and placing the patients in the hot brine that led to the establishment of brine baths at Droitwich, which have been of gradual but sure growth since that period. A correspondent of the *Daily Chronicle* writing on this subject says, "It is much too simple for some of the medical men to believe in it; when their medicine fails they send their patients to Homburg and Weisbaden. Why, are not the waters of Abana and Pharpar far better than Jordan?" Of course, they must go to Germany and France. Nantwich and Droitwich are only a few hours from London, and less from the great centres of Lancashire and Yorkshire. But the friends at Nantwich and Droitwich must not be disheartened. They will gain popularity and success by the report of those who have found relief from their afflictions. There remains one other and the crowning virtue of brine baths which you people of Crewe and we of Manchester will find the most important addition to our present character, influence, and future usefulness. One good doctor says they strengthen the backbone. I don't know whether your friends at Crewe suffer much from want of backbone, but I tell you unhesitatingly there are many in our city who do, and I urge them one and all to visit the Brine Baths at Nantwich at the earliest possible period, for depend upon it if the present competition continues we shall not only want a new stimulus to our frames, but we shall also require more moral backbone, and I may add a wider and better knowledge of geography to discover new fields for our enterprise, and more genius to devise new and beautiful goods which shall win their way into the various markets of the world against foreign competition. It has always been and I hope will continue a characteristic of our firm that we keep abreast of the times and meet the requirements of the trade in all matters pertaining to textile manufacture and clothing. We have hitherto held the foremost position as cotton manufacturers. We own what we believe to be the largest bleaching and finishing works in Great Britain, probably in Europe. We could in a few days encircle the globe with our productions. In calico, in clothing, our output is very large; in shirt fronts and shirts almost incalculable. Altogether our employés number upward of eleven thousand. We say to-night to you workpeople of Crewe, as to all our assistants in London and elsewhere, "Work on cheerfully, as you have hitherto done, and help us in the battle of competition, and enable us to maintain the ground we have now and have so long and honourably held in the front rank of the great commercial army." Our two great mottoes and trade marks are "Hard to beat," "Not the last." The latter of these is, as you know, taken from Mr. Rylands' family crest, and surely no words could be more appropriate as a commercial motto; but in other respects it is most inappropriate, for he is the last surviving merchant and manufacturer of the long list who started the race with him. He has not only outrun them in the extent of his business, but also in the length of days, and in this he is a living example to us all to work hard and live prudently. You will join me, I am sure, in wishing he may be spared for some years yet.

CHAPTER XI.

PRIZE DAY AT CHEADLE HULME ORPHAN SCHOOLS.

Mr. Spencer, after handing the prizes to the scholars, gave a short address. He said he assumed that the ladies and gentlemen present that afternoon were very closely connected with this city. The directors and managers of these noble schools were all Manchester men. He was happy to state that the movement for the education of the people had taken a deep hold on the sympathy of our citizens. As a father of a number of sons, he knew from experience the cost of education in public schools, and, judging from the excellent report, which showed the success of many of the children of this great institution, he took it that they would not be afraid to be tested against most of the schools of front rank. He rejoiced in their prosperous condition and healthy surroundings, but he could not refrain from the expression of regret that there should be one person among the higher class of Manchester warehousemen or clerks who should be so forgetful of his important duty as to neglect this grand opportunity for procuring at a small cost the inestimable boon of education and protection here provided for his children should they require them. He would remind the company and all other people that the future of this country was going to be very different to the past. The young fellows who were now enjoying the wealth of their fathers, and using their time for no practical purpose, would find society in a very altered condition twenty or thirty years hence, and unless they realised their responsibilities they would have to stand aside and let the new life, the well-educated youth of to-day, go to the front. The next generation or two would make the ground very hard for idlers. He esteemed very highly the intelligent men in all professions, but the young people in these schools would for the most part be thrown into the business world. He did not mean Manchester warehouse life, about which there was a foolish mania, but the various branches of business. What was meant by being devoted to business? Was it, as some said, a hum-drum life? He replied no. Every intelligent faculty a man possessed could find full scope in a business career, every truly philanthropic spirit, every moral instinct, every impulse of a manly soul, could there find ample room for exercise. Young people should have plenty of time for play, and a fair time for the use of the tools in the shop of the joiner or mechanic. He wished to warn them with special reference to two things. In the first, he would impress upon them the paramount importance of truthfulness, and in the second to avoid gambling. His opportunities for observation amongst young people were very considerable, and he assured them that the most horrible thing he knew of in connection with Manchester was the habit of gambling, which was carried on to an extent no one present had any conception of.

CHAPTER XII.

AFTER FIFTY YEARS.

MERCANTILE jubilees are not events of common occurrence in this strenuous and exhausting age. Few men survive the wear and tear of half a century's labour in the fields of modern commerce, and most of those upon whom fortune has smiled are well content to lay aside ambition and seek the repose which comes as the acceptable reward of prosperous toil long ere the span of their active business life has compassed fifty years. The semi-centennial of a commercial career in such a large and busy centre as Manchester implies so much in the way of long-continued and arduous effort that it may well be termed an almost unique experience; and such an experience it is now our duty and our privilege to record in connection with one of Manchester's most esteemed and most successful merchants, Mr. Reuben Spencer, whose career is biographically treated at the close of this book.

Mr. Spencer entered the house of Messrs. Rylands & Sons in 1847, a youth in his seventeenth year, and there and then began that faithful and capable discharge of the duties assigned to him which gained the approbation of his employer and secured his steady and continuous promotion. Step by step he advanced from one position to another, until he was at length invested with a power of attorney to act on behalf of the firm. From this stage in his career, in which he was for all practical purposes a partner, to the next, in which he attained the full rights and interests of partnership, was a natural and easy progression; and later still we find him taking his place among the Directors of Rylands & Sons, Limited, of which Company he is the present Chairman. He continues to take the liveliest interest in all the affairs of this great concern, and it is a remarkable fact that now, after fifty years of active and unremitting effort, accompanied in an exceptional degree by material prosperity and its attendant honours, Mr. Spencer shows no relaxation of zeal, no failure of mental or physical powers, no tendency to alter in any way his mode of life or habits of industry. His punctuality in business remains, as always, a striking characteristic of his methods, and he can boast, as few can do, that he has not deviated from his regular time of daily attendance at his office, even in these later years when the claims of nature and the demands of social and public duties might easily furnish excuses for some loosening of the reins of self-imposed discipline. Mr. Spencer has been favoured with the health and strength essential to one who sets an example of constant application to work, and the only occasion upon which he was absent from business for any appreciable length of time through illness occurred nearly forty years ago, when an attack of English cholera confined him to the house for the brief space of a day and a-half. The youth of 1847 has thus passed through all the stages of progress appertaining to a great commercial house, and the other day, as head of the immense concern in which he once served as a subordinate, he had the pleasure and satisfaction of fitly commemorating his "Golden Jubilee" by entertaining eleven hundred employes of the house of Rylands, which employed less than one hundred assistants in its warehouse at the date of his entering the establishment.

On the occasion of the memorable gathering just referred to, Mr. Spencer's friends had the gratification of hearing from his own lips the statement that he still felt physically equal to the discharge of any duty, and mentally more capable than ever of meeting the demands made upon his powers by the gigantic business over which he at present presides. At the same time—having attained the distinction of a commercial jubilee, and fulfilled his destiny as one of the leading spirits in the business life of modern Manchester—Mr. Spencer may now be more ready to see the force of the advice tendered him from time to time by his colleagues and other friends, that he should husband his strength, and avail himself more liberally of the means of maintaining his bodily health and vigour. Though to such a man as the Chairman of Messrs. Rylands & Sons, Limited, there is a peculiar force in Cowper's line, "Absence of occupation is not rest"; yet a manner of repose is the most fitting crown and sequel to all good and honest work, and there are many who think that such repose has been splendidly earned by Mr. Reuben Spencer. In his own interests, as well as in those of the house which owes so much to his fifty years of unwearying labour, he might, with the fullest justification, begin at this auspicious time to relax in some degree the efforts by which he has raised himself to his present eminence, sustained in his own person and firm the prestige of the Manchester trade, and made his career in this great city a pattern to all who have the spirit to emulate and the resolution to follow and copy so worthy an exemplar.

Chapter XIII.

MR. REUBEN SPENCER'S JUBILEE.

THE directors of Rylands & Sons, Limited, are becoming noted for their jubilee celebrations. Mr. Reuben Spencer, the esteemed chairman of the board, completed his fiftieth year with the firm on the 10th of this month, and the event was celebrated on Saturday, when Mr. Spencer entertained the male employés of the Manchester warehouse and the managers, and the heads of departments of the various mills and works at the Belle Vue Gardens, on Saturday, February 13th, 1897. There were about 1,100 persons present, and the proceedings were of an enthusiastic character. In the afternoon there was a football match between the employés of the various establishments of the firm, and during the evening Mr. and Mrs. Spencer were the recipients of a gift to commemorate the jubilee. The female employés were received by Mrs. Spencer at her residence, Darley Hall, Whalley Range. Amongst those present at Belle Vue on Saturday were Mr. W. Carnelley, Mr. W. D. Gloyne, Mr. T. Harker, Mr. W.

DARLEY HALL. RESIDENCE OF MR. REUBEN SPENCER.

ENTRANCE HALL.

Linnell, and Mr. J. Wright (directors), Mr. Norman Spencer, Mr. Douglas Spencer, the Rev. Allen Spencer, Mr. J. E. Yates, Mr. Arnold Linnell, Mr. B. Goodfellow, and all the buyers and heads of departments from the warehouse and works in Manchester.

The presentation consisted of a handsome silver tea and coffee service, chased in the Renaissance style, with a kettle to match and a massive tray, which was engraved as follows: "Presented, with the accompanying silver service, to Reuben Spencer, Esq., J.P., by the employés in the Manchester warehouses, also the mills and works, of Rylands & Sons, Limited, as a mark of their esteem, and in celebration of his jubilee in connection with the firm. Manchester, February 13th, 1897." The whole service, which had been specially manufactured by Messrs. Elkington & Co., Limited, of Manchester, was contained in a handsome oak case. There was also a facsimile of the tea service on a smaller scale for Mrs. Spencer. This, with a charming silver hot-water jug, was contained in a morocco case richly lined with velvet.

Mr. H. Ashcroft asked the acceptance by Mr. Spencer of an illuminated address and service of silver from the employés as a token of their high regard for him personally, and to show their appreciation of his character as a business man. Mr. Spencer's wonderful energy, prompt action, perseverance under difficulties, and undeviating punctuality

DRAWING ROOM.

were well known to them. He had subordinated personal ambition to the interests of Rylands & Sons. Municipal and parliamentary honours had been offered and declined. Had he been so disposed he might have been to-day the president of the Manchester Chamber of Commerce, a position only given to gentlemen of acknowledged ability and position. This was the eighth half-century celebration in connection with the firm. The first was the jubilee of Mr. Rylands in 1873, Mr. Meadows in 1884, Mr. Robert Davies in 1886, Mr. Carnelley in 1890, Mr. Hoggan in 1895, and Messrs. Harker and Knott last year. Four of the eight were present at this gathering. This was a record unprecedented in the history of any commercial house in the world. The length of service to the firm of the committee who had the presentation in hand averaged thirty six years. He could readily find fifty others whose connection with the firm was equally as long. This was a remarkable proof of the spirit of brotherhood which characterized the members of the staff, and which added much to the success of the vast concern with which they were all identified. Mr. Ashcroft read the following address, signed by the members of the committee and 1,100 contributors :—

"We the buyers, managers, salesmen, clerks, and others employed by Messrs. Rylands & Sons, Limited, in the Manchester warehouse, New High Street; Dacca Twist Company, Faulkner Street, Manchester, also at Gorton, Wigan, Bolton, and Swinton Mills, Gidlow Collieries, and Longford, Medlock, Heapey, Chorley

DRAWING ROOM, ANOTHER VIEW.

and Crewe works, desire to offer to you our united and hearty congratulations on the occasion of your completion of fifty years' faithful service in the great firm with which it is also our pleasure to be identified. We sincerely trust that you may continue to enjoy that measure of health and strength which will enable you for many years yet to come to occupy the important position you have so long and honourably filled, and thus to contribute, as hitherto, to the steady and most satisfactory management which has consolidated the company, and raised it to such an eminent position among the many colossal enterprises of which our country justly boasts. As a further recognition of this, your 'commercial golden wedding,' and as a tribute of our respect, admiration, and esteem, we beg your acceptance of the accompanying pieces of silver, which, however, merely reflect the spontaneous good-will of each contributor. We hope that this memento may prove a source of life-long satisfaction and pleasure to Mrs. Spencer, yourself, and each member of your family."

    H. ASHCROFT (Chairman).
    H. A. SOUTHWORTH (Treasurer).

W. F. BEWLEY.	NATHAN MEADOWS.
HENRY BRIGHTMORE.	J. PONTEFRACT.
J. W. CLEGG.	ROBT. H. POTTER.
THOS. B. COOPER.	NICHOLAS H. SIBLY.
CHARLES DERNALEY.	MATTHEW TOMLINSON.
JNO. EDWARDS.	THOS. B. WALTON.
J. JOHNSON.	

    THOS. KENDALL and
    S. J. TENANT } Hon. Secretaries.

Messrs. Nathan Meadows and T. B. Cooper, old servants of the firm, also spoke a few words of congratulation to Mr. Spencer.

Mr. W. F. Bewley said he had much pleasure in asking Mr. Spencer to receive, on behalf of his wife, a silver afternoon tea-service. They ventured to hope she might find in that little token of regard an abiding memento of a happy celebration. (Applause.)

Messrs. H. A. Southworth and J. W. Clegg having also offered their congratulations,

Mr. Spencer, in reply, said: "This is a moment of extreme joy—the foundation of a permanent pleasure to me and my children to the third generation. These emblems of beauty in design and of usefulness in the home will be a perpetual remembrance of kindness felt and expressed towards me, showing you can forget little irritations occurring through life, and courteously and generously acknowledge the services I have been able to render during a period of fifty years in the house of Rylands & Sons. I have been a youth, a young and middle-aged man amongst you, and I have now to acknowledge advancing years. At no time, whether in youth or manhood, whether as servant, partner, or director, have I been charged with want of attention to business, with want of punctuality, or with a desire to shirk responsibility. This is the negative side of my business character. The affirmative you have appreciated, and in word and deed have been kind beyond my expectation and my deserts. Young men, allow me to take this opportunity to offer a few words of advice and kindly admonition. I never allowed my expenditure to exceed my income; never gave myself to gambling or trying to secure another man's money without giving labour of some kind for it, and never since I left my home did I forget the duties of a child to a parent, or, according to my light and my understanding, the duties of a parent to a child. I was blessed with a noble, courageous, and loving mother,

DINING ROOM.

and still more with a tender, affectionate, and wise woman as a wife, nor will I omit to mention my deep obligation to Mr. Rylands, near to whom I worked for many long years, and to whose inspiring words and fine business example my indebtedness is greater than I can express. He has gone, leaving a great mark behind. My time will soon expire, my work will be finished, and my desire is to leave some little mark upon the institutions and the commerce of my adopted county. (Applause.) After saying all this, do not suppose I have made no mistakes or blunders in my life. I have made many, and some very foolish ones. A number of things I could improve. The trouble and annoyance which have arisen from some mistakes I could avoid, but yet such are the varied influences at work, and in so many ways are the physical and mental powers affected, that I am afraid I, and all others, would make equally great irregularities if we had a similar period to pass through again. I will try to feel thankful that I have passed through so many years with such an average of pleasure and success. We are all more or less wise from experience, and see matters in a very different light, but human nature continues to be liable to errors and slips, and so it will be to the end of time. You have to-day made a lasting mark upon my family record, which will endure in memory and in gratitude, for a time beyond which any of us can live. I came into this city more than fifty years ago. I had no extra-

BILLIARD ROOM.

ordinarily favourable surroundings. It was not my lot to be born in a noble or wealthy house. I was not helped by wealthy friends or parents. My special wealth was a fair education and a sound mind in a healthy body. I never ill-used the latter by bad habits, except it be those of working very long hours and for many years in a terribly bad atmosphere. I am glad to say my health to-day is as good as ever it was, and though I cannot join you in a game of football or cricket or tennis, I can rejoice with you in witnessing the games. In all that pertains to the administration of this business concern, and helping to make it profitable and useful, I will take my place by your side, whether that place be at the top, the middle, or the bottom of the ladder, and I will try in future to make my influence felt for good, as by your testimony you acknowledge I have done in the past. Possibly someone in the audience is asking, 'Mr. Spencer, what was the house like when you first knew it?' Well, it was comparatively small. We had then less than a hundred employés in the warehouse. We have now 1,200 in the Manchester warehouse, and about 1,000 in London and Liverpool, with 10,000 in our various works, or a total of about 12,000. We had at that time three or four travellers. Now we have seventy at least, beside our foreign agents. We had then fewer than ten departments. At present we have forty in Manchester and the same in London. Our turnover was then measured by scores of thousands of pounds per annum, plus the output of our two mills and bleach-works; now it is many millions of pounds every year. We then dealt only in heavy goods. We now furnish a house with everything required, and supply men, women, and children with every article needed for personal adornment, even to the watch and chain, gold links, studs, cycles, and the most delicate articles of ladies' attire. We then had two mills and a small bleach works. We have now the largest bleach works in the country, and sixteen mills, works, and warehouses devoted to the production and distribution of cotton, woollen, and other goods in almost endless variety. We go down into the dark chambers below the surface of the ground and bring up the black diamonds which illumine the hearth at home and produce steam to move the machinery in our works. We make some and repair most of our machinery; we make our own boxes and cases for packing purposes and for our own use in the salerooms; we do our own printing and make our pattern cards; and we make first-class buyers and travellers, clerks, and salesmen—not the ordinary sort, but men of excellence alike in character and capacity, without whom we should not be what we are to-day. (Applause.) What more can I say? We have accomplished great things in the last fifty years. Some of your directors have been at the helm all the way, and some have come to these high duties later. We have all done our level best, and the result is something which warrants the directors, buyers, travellers, agents, clerks, salesmen, and each one of you, in feeling some degree of satisfaction, if not of pride, in having brought the concern to its present position. We can say our turnover exceeds that of any firm in the textile trade, with a profit which satisfies all our shareholders. As civilisation extends, and the population increases, so by an unalterable law of authority in human existence the wants and needs of the people will increase in a still larger proportion, and in some measure there should be an increase in business in every well-organized and wisely-administered concern. When I cease to feel the power to meet the new demands, to show signs of decreasing capacity or indisposition to increase, then I must, and will, move from the front form. This may come sooner than some of us expect, but I trust you will allow me to take a side seat with less to do, so that I may not rust out. We are, I believe, to-day the greatest textile house in the world. I claim to have had a modest influence and share in the building of it. I had a magnificent example. I exercised my eyes, my heart, and my hands, and I rejoice to find you willing to acknowledge that my labour has not been in vain. Excuse me rejoicing in the manifest approval of my services expressed in your kindly words and deeds. If ever in my heart I felt I could say a kind word to the men of Rylands and Sons, it it to-day. To anyone to whom I have in time past said an unkind word, I tell you it was not from an unkind heart, but from a good motive, though it may have appeared otherwise. Never from malice aforethought have I spoken or done you a wrong intentionally. In the administration of a large business and the guidance of a number of men differences must arise, but in this I feel as I do about travelling. I hate the sea, but I would go to Australia to-morrow if duty called me. I hate wrangling and hard words, but I will boldly and fearlessly speak to any man and tell him my thoughts, not in malice, but according to the depth and strength of my convictions and the light I possess. One and all, I thank you again from my heart for the noble present you have made to me and my good wife and family.". (Applause.)

The Rev. Allan Spencer spoke on behalf of his mother, and thanked them for the gifts. This day's proceedings, he said, would be one of the landmarks in their family history. (Applause.)

The remainder of the evening was devoted to songs and music by the members of the Rylands' Brass and String Bands (under the conductorship of Mr. R. Jackson), the Orchestral Society (under the conductorship of Mr. G. H. Johnson), and the Memorial Club assisting in the evening's entertainment. Mr. W. Ashton and his glee party also added to the harmony.

The testimonial to Mr. Spencer is engrossed on vellum, the illumination being in the quaint Celtic style, the opening pages being especially rich in design and colour. It contains four pages of text, to which are appended the signatures of the presentation committee and the names of 1,100 subscribers connected with the various departments of Messrs. Rylands & Sons' offices, warehouses, mills, and works. Mr. Spencer's portrait, carefully drawn in sepia, forms a pleasing frontispiece, and opposite the text pages appear eleven sepia views of the chief buildings of the firm. The address is bound in rich scarlet levant morocco with a special Celtic border inlaid, and a sunken vellum panel containing monogram "R. S." in the centre of the front cover, richly illuminated in blue, terra-cotta, and gold; the volume is enclosed in a purple morocco padded box, forming a magnificent work of art, the production of Messrs. Palmer, Howe & Co., Manchester.

Chapter XIV.

THE LIVERPOOL BRANCH'S TRIBUTE.

MR. Reuben Spencer's jubilee was celebrated in a similar manner at the Liverpool Branch on Monday last, when Mr. Milne presided over a large gathering of the staff. The Chairman made some complimentary remarks as to Mr. Spencer's commercial and public character, and spoke feelingly of his close connexion with the house, and of his courtesy and healthy influence over all the men since its commencement up to the present, his oversight and management of the old warehouse, and the purchase and transfer to the present new eligible premises, which were a credit to the firm to own and to occupy, thoroughly equipped and furnished as they were for a large business.

Mr. Stephenson then rose, and after stating the circumstances under which he was first engaged (now twenty-three years ago) by Mr. Spencer, he referred to the happy relations which existed between the employés and the directors, and of Mr. Spencer in particular, and of his own pleasant position as the oldest representative the firm had in Liverpool. He then uncovered a beautiful and chaste silver bowl and a richly illuminated address bound in elegant form. He read the address and the names of the employés, and presented them to Mr. Spencer. He said the bowl could not be said to be the flowing bowl; it was not filled with liquid often referred to in such articles, but he could assure Mr. Spencer it was filled to overflowing with the highest sentiment and the best wishes of every man in the house. They all wished him long life, and that he would continue to exercise his ripe judgment and valuable experience in the interests of the firm with which he had been so long and so honourably connected, and of which he is the present chairman.

Mr. Spencer, in responding, said: "Many of your remarks are too kind, but I know you are sincere, and this evidence of your feeling in the present before me is most gratifying. A considerable number of you have been with the firm many years, and we have been in close contact all through, and have enjoyed mutual confidence and support. It is true this is the last established of the three houses, but this is not your fault or the firm's. It is the circumstances which we could not control; we could have done more on a wider field of operation, but this we can and will say emphatically, we have done our best where we are, and I am conceited enough to think and to say few, if any, could have done more or better. We are in the front, and there we mean to stay. Liverpool is a grand city, and has a greater future before it, and we hope to be still more worthy of our position and to enjoy a greater share of the business done in the city and district. Our premises are as complete and well equipped, and in as good a position as it is possible to find. Our stock, both in value and quantity, will be maintained according to the necessities of the place. We may truly use the phrase, "We have the men and the money too." Only demand and your requirements shall be promptly met. Much has been said about years of service, and, of course, special reference has been made to my own. This has given rise, in my mind, to reflection as to the mode of measuring time which is very interesting. Strictly interpreted, a year is a measure of time definite and fixed, but the term has a significance far beyond the rigid interpretation. When you speak of a child three years of age you feel, and you desire it to be understood, the child has passed beyond infancy, and has become interesting and observant, and so on as he or she advances to eight, twelve, or eighteen; if a male, by that age he generally matures so fast that in his own estimation he could rule the British Squadron as easily and confidently as he tries to teach and direct the thoughts of his parents. If a girl, then she assumes some aspects and characteristics of a woman, but with all the grace and beauty of carriage of demeanour of a lady, and charms any circle into which she enters; but it is not so much the meaning of the word "year" as applied to youth to which I desire to call your attention; it is to men of mature years, say fifty and upwards. When you speak of the age of such a person you have the thought of a man of experience, of capacity, of some power or force of character which could not be obtained except by long labour, and of course there is much truth and propriety in the feeling, but the word "year" means vastly more than this. A man to-day, aided by the various modern appliances and his increased intellectual power, can do as much real work in one day as his predecessor, say sixty or seventy years ago, could have performed in three or four days. Yea, in some departments of life he could accomplish in a week as much for the general help and benefit of mankind as fifty men could have performed in the same period in the last century, and so when you speak of a man of years you mean much more than is generally understood. You mean all that experience and power which comes from natural genius and high gifts from varied reading, and the great capacity which some possess of appropriating and applying the good and ripe thoughts and discoveries of other men. I must now bring my remarks to a close, and again thank you very sincerely for your kind words, and in the name of my family for your handsome present. I can assure you they will be highly and deservedly appreciated by us all. I must say here as to the larger gathering of something near 1,200 who met me a few days ago from our parent house in Manchester, "God bless us all, and preserve us in unity and in successful labour for many years to come."

Mr. Carnelley, one of the directors, was present, and spoke a few cheering words to the young men, showing what had been done in Manchester, in London, and lastly in Liverpool, and said as these celebrations must come to an end, so his period of service, as well as those of Mr. Spencer and others, must come to an end, and it was for them to see which could use their experience to advantage, having regard to their future positions.

Chapter XV.

MR. REUBEN SPENCER'S JUBILEE.

PRESENTATION BY HIS CO-DIRECTORS.

IN further commemoration of Mr. Spencer's Jubilee, he was entertained at dinner on Saturday, February 20, at the Albion Hotel, Manchester, by his colleagues on the directorate of Rylands & Sons, Limited.

Mr. Carnelley, who presided, spoke in affectionate terms of the long friendship which he and Mr. Spencer had enjoyed in the service of the same firm, he having been with the house since 1840, when it consisted of four departments and only twenty-eight employés, and now Mr. Spencer had completed his fifty years of service. They were met that day to honour him and to give him some lasting token of their esteem; they also desired to give expression to their high appreciation of Mrs. Spencer, and to offer her their sincere congratulations on this happy occasion. Mr. Carnelley then asked Mr. Spencer's acceptance of a drawing-room clock and sidepieces, a pair of vases, and a silver entrée dish; and also handed to Mr. Spencer a pair of bracelets for Mrs. Spencer, with a hope that she might long wear them, and that they might be handed down as heirlooms for many years to come.

Mr. Dunford said although he had not the privilege of the long acquaintance with Mr. Spencer that others present could claim, still he might say that he was known to him by repute for some few years before he entered the company's employ. It afforded him the greatest pleasure to offer him his hearty congratulations on completion of fifty years' service with Rylands & Sons, Limited, whom he had served so faithfully and with such distinction, and he sincerely trusted that for many years they might have the benefit of his valuable experience.

Mr. J. Edmondson expressed his pleasure at being present on such an occasion, and his still greater pleasure at seeing Mr. Spencer apparently as full of energy and determination to go ahead as ever. He remembered that at the general meeting of the company, held a few weeks previously, in response to some remarks by a shareholder about his coming jubilee, Mr. Spencer then said that he felt almost as good a man as ever, and capable of a few more years of active service in the firm. He earnestly hoped this might be the case, and that they might long continue to have the benefit of his great experience, close application to business, and undoubted capacity.

Mr. Gloyne said that the keynote of the day's proceedings had been given him by one of their London friends in the earlier part of the day. He had said that he came from London to render "honour to whom honour was due." It was with this idea that they had assembled and endeavoured to do honour to their guest, asking his acceptance of the articles now presented to him as a token of their regard and esteem. It was now more than forty years ago since he first made Mr. Spencer's acquaintance, and it was a very rare occurrence to find a man with such energy left in him and used for the conduct and improvement of such a concern after so long a period spent in its service. He did not intend to say that others present had not worked in the interest of the firm, but that was not the point for them to consider. All they were doing at present was to present their feelings of respect and admiration for the amount of good work done in that direction by their guest. He could wish that Mr. Spencer would take things more easily sometimes—take more time for rest and recreation—but trusted that he would be long spared to throw the same energy into the business, and that Mrs. Spencer and family might, with him, have many years in which to enjoy the different manifestations of regard and esteem now being made to them.

Mr. Harker said it gave him great pleasure to be here on that occasion to congratulate Mr. Spencer on having completed fifty years of valuable service in connection with the firm of Rylands & Sons,

Limited. He also shared the pleasure it afforded them in handing to Mr. Spencer what they thought would be accepted as a token of regard which might be handed down from generation to generation. He trusted Mr. Spencer might long be spared to the firm with which they were connected, and that the energy and perseverance which had marked Mr. Spencer's life in business might be his for years to come.

Mr. Linnell said: It is a great pleasure to me to join my colleagues in expressing to you our appreciation of the efforts you have bestowed so lavishly in promoting the prosperity of Rylands & Sons (Limited), and I congratulate you that after fifty years wear and tear of active business life, to-day finds you in good health both physical and mental, and we are glad to know that your heart is now as true and loyal to the best interests of Rylands & Sons, Limited, as ever it was. The testimonials you received last Saturday and last Monday, and those which you have received to-day, cannot but affect you deeply, and chiefly because they are the freewill offerings of fellow-workers, who, knowing your long and arduous labours during the fifty years you have been connected with the company, desire to express to you their appreciation of those labours—not in words only, but in forms which we hope will be pleasant reminders for many years to come, both to you and those near and dear to you, of the esteem in which you are held. And I feel sure you will value the gifts so much the more by the knowledge of the motives which prompted them. If Mrs. Spencer had been with us to-day it would have been a great pleasure to her to see how high you stand in our esteem, and if you carried into your home life some of those cares and anxieties which are inseparable from the position you occupy, and thereby interfered somewhat with her own pleasure and enjoyment, she would now feel some satisfaction in knowing that her patience and self-denial, and your laborious days spent in the discharge of important duties, have won the appreciation of those who know how to value the sacrifices you have both made. A jubilee is a time when it is convenient and instructive to look back on past failures and successes and review our own work and that of past colleagues. I shall not attempt this, because there are some here who can go back much farther than I can. They can trace the progress of the concern from small beginnings and tell of its numerous struggles, successful ventures, and departed men, who bore bravely the heat and burden of the day, and to whom we, and the company we represent, are greatly indebted for the proud and honourable position we now occupy. John Rylands, Robert Beveridge Hoggan, and James Horrocks are three honoured names in the history of Rylands & Sons, Limited. It has been our privilege to work by their side. They were men of strong convictions, enduring capacity for work, impelled by irresistible energy and determination, and having confidence in themselves they inspired the confidence of others. And although the last-named did not reach the unique position of having a jubilee, we can, all the same, speak to his worth. He laboured with a constancy and devotion worthy of the highest praise. I join heartily and sincerely in the expressions of good-will which have been conveyed to you to-day, and share the hope that you will long continue to discharge the duties of your position, and retain that appetite for work and determination to do it, which have distinguished you in the past.

Mr. Mitchener also spoke in a very kindly manner, and referred at some length to the growth of the London business.

Mr. Wright expressed the pleasure it afforded him to be present on that most interesting occasion, and to add his words of congratulation with those of his brother directors to Mr. Spencer on the attainment of his jubilee with their grand old firm. It was not given to many men to see such a term of service—in fact it was unique—and this he said in face of the fact that they in Rylands & Sons, Limited, had celebrated no less than eight of such terms of service in late years, for in these jubilees their firm stood almost alone. How proud their late governor, Mr. Rylands, would have been had he been spared to see such gatherings as the one now held to commemorate fifty years' faithful services of gentlemen he had chosen in their youth to serve him in building up the business they have now to direct, and what a feeling of pleasure it must give Mr. Spencer, and those left on the board who had been connected for so long a time together, to look back and remember how from small beginnings it had become the great concern it is to-day—from tens of thousands to hundreds of thousands, and from hundreds of thousands to many millions in turnover. Mr. Wright said it was now approaching thirty years since he became acquainted with Mr. Spencer in Rylands & Sons, Limited, and well remembered his introduction to him, and added he had only one regret in coming to the firm, and that was that he had not the opportunity fifteen years earlier of joining it, for he felt sure it would have been to his great benefit; and, more than that, he would have been so many years nearer his own jubilee. Mr. Gloyne stood the next on the list, with about ten years yet before him before that event would be accomplished, which he (Mr. Wright) trusted it would be, and he himself intended to do all in his power to see his own, although so much more distant. Mr. Wright concluded his remarks by again warmly congratulating Mr. Spencer.

Mr. Spencer, in reply, said: Mr. Carnelley and Brother Directors,—Before replying to the kind words which have been addressed to me, I must first gratefully and heartily acknowledge your kindness in again electing me to the position of chairman of the company. It is evidence at once of your good-will and of your confidence that I shall devote my best energy and capacity to the service of the firm, and shall try to avoid any action which should imperil the traditions of the office or the honour and fame of the great company whose affairs we have to administer. I am greatly pleased on behalf of myself and family to receive this unexpectedly munificent gift from the board in conjunction with Mrs. Rylands. To say the clock and ornaments for the mantel are great in value, artistic in design and form, that the bracelets are handsome and suitable for any lady, and the silver dish most appropriate for the purpose it is intended to serve, is to use words that are not fully representative of my feeling. You and I know there is an unwritten and unwriteable expression of feeling which words cannot convey, but which kind and generous hearts can interpret and understand. It is through this medium I must express my gratitude to you. Gentlemen, it is true some of us have been very closely associated with the firm for fifty years, and others for a shorter period, but, sirs, service is not only measured by years, but by capacity, ability, and willingness to discharge the onerous duties devolving upon men in our position, who have to administer a great concern employing 12,000 people, and managing a property which in various forms amounts to £4,000,000 sterling. We have all done our best, and the result is before the commercial world, and I say with something more than satisfaction that the pleasant relations which exist between us and our army of workpeople, with the 2,000 assistants in the various warehouses, the 20,000 customers on our books, and the shareholders in the company, all combine to give us a unique position in this great commercial nation, and in Europe. It is true our capital is large, our *clientèle* a great one; and these give us large power and authority in the markets. All the more credit to us, and to the staff as a whole. But, brother directors, we have not done yet. All this experience and acquired power should be aids to further achievements, and this not necessarily to the disparagement of other good and true men. It is estimated that the world has a population of about 1,500 millions of human beings, who want food and clothing, and the proportion of comforts demanded by the increasing population of civilized people is greatly in excess of the number in their old conditions. A million of educated and industrial people want five or ten times the quantity of material that a million of uncivilized people require. There is a great deal of room in the business world, and our plan should be to do our best, and find no fault with others who do the same, if they do it honestly. I will say no more. I thank you most heartily and sincerely on behalf of my family, who I know will highly appreciate this magnificent and valuable gift, which will give untold pleasure to us all. If I wanted an incentive this certainly would put new life and purpose in me.

CHAPTER XVI.

MR. REUBEN SPENCER'S JUBILEE.

FURTHER PRESENTATIONS.

LAST week in Manchester and Liverpool the celebration of Mr. Reuben Spencer's jubilee was commemorated — that is to say, his completion of fifty years' service with Messrs. Rylands and Sons, Limited. Since then, the festivities have been continued in London, and on Wednesday, February 24th, an address and a gold watch and chain were presented to Mr. Spencer by a number of his old friends in the London house. The ceremony took place at the Cannon Street Hotel after tea, to which the subscribers had been invited. In the course of the proceedings a letter was received from Mrs. Rylands, in which she expressed her desire to join with those present in expressing her congratulations to Mr. Spencer, and wishing him many years of active life in connection with the firm. The chair was taken by Mr. G. W. C. Kirkham, the oldest buyer in the London house. He was supported by Mr. Carnelley and Mr. Harker (themselves famous

" jubileers "), and Mr. Mitchener and Mr. Dunford, London directors. Nearly the whole of the subscribers were present. Tea having been partaken of—

The Chairman said: It is only right that I should tell you that I am not in this position to-night of my own seeking, but because the committee have done me the great honour of asking me to preside for the fourth time at a director's jubilee. This position would have been better filled by one of those who have been associated with Mr. Spencer longer, for though his name has been a household word since his manhood, still I have only been with him in this great business of Rylands and Sons, Limited, some twenty-four years. I will, however, yield to none in high appreciation of the gentleman whom we have met to-night to honour; and we have done right in being determined to honour him, for has he not filled up the whole of this fifty years with credit, and this being the year of Jubilee, how could we do otherwise than show him how high he stands in our esteem. Then does he not hail from what, to many of us, is our native city, a city that is known and respected wherever trade and commerce, or the English language has gone, and that great business city has done him great honour. Amongst its financiers, amongst its merchants, amongst its manufacturers, and amongst its men of progress, it has always placed him in the first rank. Having already said so much about the jubilee previously, it is a difficult matter to go over the ground without repeating myself. But let us for a few moments just hark back and try to think what this fifty years of service means, and we see Mr. Spencer entering the warehouse as a boy, and for many years we see him laying hold of its various details, one at a time—just as a man putting a warp into a loom, one thread at a time, so he took them up—and, when he had mastered it and his hands were full, how, when he was still a very young man, our grand old founder, Mr. John Rylands, made him joint master of what was one of the largest businesses of its kind; and I need hardly tell you how he and his able colleagues have since carried it forward, until to-day it is the envy of the textile world. I noticed that the American Ambassador said the other evening, at a banquet given previous to his departure, "That it had ever been his aim to try and knit together the two great peoples of England and America"—a grand object; and no doubt this will go down with his name to posterity. And thus it ever is. A general returns from a short, successful campaign; a traveller returns from his travels; this man and that returns from various expeditions; and they are banqueted, and feasted, and lionised. But, gentlemen, our company is returning from a campaign that has lasted not two, or ten, or twenty, but for fifty years; and it is right and proper that we should rejoice and be glad, and that we should come with flags and banners flying, and drums beating and trumpets sounding, for we are returning from a successful campaign of many battles and dangers overcome, without wounded in the van, and with our captain unscathed at our head. I would not detract for one moment from the honour that belongs to our great men, be they soldiers, sailors, professors, merchants, or others, for it must be grand to be a great man, to have gained by energy and perseverance the topmost step of the ladder to which we had put our hand and foot. But how much grander must it be to a good and a great man to be able, from the pinnacle to which that man has climbed, to look back and feel honestly that he is leaving the world better for having lived therein! Kirke White sums up both positions thus—

"Where are the heroes of the ages past? Where the brave chieftains? Where the mighty ones that flourished in the infancy of years? All to the grave gone down: on their fallen fame, exultation, mocking at the pride of man, sits grim forgetfulness. The warrior's arm lies nerveless on the pillow of its shame, hushed is his stormy voice, and quenched the blaze of his red eyeballs. Yesterday, and his name was mighty on the earth: to-day, 'tis what?—The meteor of the night that flashed unnoticed. Where are concealed the days which have elapsed?—Hid in the mighty caverns of the past, they rise upon us only to appal, with indistinct and half-glimpsed images, misty, gigantic, huge, obscure, remote. But the good man's hope lies far, far beyond the sway of tempest or the furious sweep of mortal desolation. He beholds, unapprehensive, the gigantic stride of rampant ruin, or the unstable waves of dark vicissitude."

Sir, I trust when the annals of this colossal undertaking of Rylands and Sons, Limited, are written, that the historian will be able to write of you, and each of your able colleagues, and of us the rank and file—

"Their work well done, their race well run, their crowns well won; here let them rest."

THE ADDRESS.

Mr. J. C. Later, buyer of the muslin department, who has served the house in London and Manchester for a period of thirty-three years, was asked to read the address, which runs as follows:—

"To REUBEN SPENCER, ESQ., J.P.

"DEAR SIR,—The Buyers, Chief Clerks, and Representatives of the London House of Rylands & Sons, Limited, whose names are written opposite, desire most heartily to congratulate you on the occasion of your Jubilee, and ask you to accept a Gold Watch and Chain as a Souvenir of this interesting event. We greatly admire the wisdom, dignity, and power with which you have for so many years assisted to direct and control the affairs of the great mercantile concern to which we have the honour to belong, as well as in the promotion of the general interests of British commerce. We also highly appreciate your efforts in the sacred cause of Charity, your interests in the great work of Education, and your desire to promote healthful recreation and thrift amongst the employés of our famous House. That the years to come may bring you continued prosperity, good health, and long life is our most earnest prayer.—February, 1897."

The names of the subscribers are as follow:—

Messrs. J. J. Ablett, W. Armstrong, P. Burgess, P. A. Brooks, J. W. Booth, W. R. Coway, H. Coles, W. J. Cooke, J. Dakers, J. Durant, C. W. Edwards, G. C. Fisher, T. Gow, R. Greenhalgh, J. M. Gindell, R. Hartshorn, S. R. Hallam, W. Harrold, W. Hoggan, J. Humphries, J. Hunter, T. N. Hubble, R. J. Jackson, H. F. Jones, W. Keen, S. W. C. Kirkham, J. W. Kirkham, F. R. King, F. King, J. C. Knight, C. Langridge, J. Lawson, S. T. Liddiard, J. C. Later, R. A. Martin, H. McLean, E. C. Morgan, J. S. Murison, K. Nicholas, J. Pettit, F. R. Pateman, E. Prescott, J. W. Pinkerton, D. Rayner, J. A. Scott, F. Swallow, F. Smith, W. Snell, J. W. Snupe, A. Tawell, J. Williams, A. E. Wells, R. Whittaker, J. L. Wilson.

The Presentation.

Mr. S. Barratt, in making the presentation of the gold watch and chain, remarked that the total length of service of the 55 subscribers amounted to 929 years. Four of them had served the house for a period of over 30 years each, while twenty of the others could show a service of over 20 years each. He begged Mr. Spencer to wear the watch on State occasions in honour of the subscribers, and in due course to leave it as a precious heirloom to his family. He also read the following jubilee ode in honour of the occasion :—

R emember not the years of toil and strife,
E ach loving heart should learn the joy of life ;
U nto the good and pure sweet days are given,
B est fitted to prepare the soul for Heaven ;
E ach future year may joy and blessing bring,
N or will we cease your noble fame to sing.

S ing, joyous Muse ! the praises of our Chief,
P roclaim aloud the banishment of grief ;
E ach noble voice join in the happy song,
N ight unto night the welcome strain prolong ;
C hant forth a sweet and merry note of glee,
E ach welcome guest rejoice and happy be :
R ejoice ! it is the year of Jubilee.

Mr. J. A. Scott, speaking on behalf of the buyers, said:—It gives me great pleasure to add my quota to what has already been so ably expressed by the friends who have preceded me. The very fact alone of our honoured guest and host being associated with the firm for the long period of fifty years, it is needless to say, gives him an enviable reputation. In Mr. Spencer we recognise a man of many parts, not only as author of some most useful and instructive books, but to him are we in great part indebted as being one of the prime movers in our recreation and thrift fund,—institutions, gentlemen, which, permit me to say, are far-reaching in their effect for good, extending and diffusing as they do to the healthful exercise and social enjoyment of the employés generally. Gentlemen, the student of history may go back to the ancient times of Pericles, wade through history's pages right down to the Elizabethan period, and still on to the Victorian era, and even there I venture to say he will not find a parallel case with our own. He will not find in the textile trade a house whose successful history and volume of business will compare with Rylands & Sons'; and surely it is to the able administrations of this grand old firm that we are indebted for this splendid monument, men whose devotion to duty and example will stand out as beacon lights to the generations that follow. It is in the association of men who are wiser and more experienced than ourselves that we become inspired and invigorated, for they enhance our own knowledge, enlarge our field of wisdom, and we profit by their experience. (Addressing Mr. Spencer.) In mingling my hearty congratulations on this very happy and unique occasion, the celebration of your jubilee, permit me to express the hope that you may be blessed with a goodly store of health, so that you may enjoy to the full the rich fruits of your long and honourable career.

Mr. John Humphreys, the veteran town traveller, congratulated Mr. Spencer on behalf of the travellers, and said that there were no men more loyal to the firm than the buyers, clerks, and travellers of the London house.

Mr. Carnelley was proud to be present to hear the speeches. He warmly praised the spirit of unity amongst the directors and buyers, which was one great cause of their strength. He hoped Mr. Spencer would be long spared to serve the house.

Mr. Harker warmly eulogised Mr. Spencer, remarking that they had been boys together.

Mr. Mitchener remarked that this was a unique occasion. There were three gentlemen present who had each served fifty years with the firm. They had been as good trees planted in good soil.

Mr. Dunford paid a hearty tribute of praise to the character of the gentleman they were met to honour.

Mr. Spencer's Speech.

Mr. Spencer replied as follows :—In reply to your various kind remarks—much too kind—I can only say I value very highly the beautiful gold watch, chain, and address which are before me, and sincerely appreciate the generous spirit which has prompted you to make this handsome present, and for the courtesy and good feeling which breathes through every speech and every line of the address. Gentlemen, this is an incentive and encouragement to all to do their part in life's work in the best way they can. In reference to my service to the company, I can truly say that the duties which have fallen to my lot have been discharged to the best of my ability. I found as years rolled on my responsibilities increased, and I also soon discovered that the office of administrator in an ever-growing concern was an onerous one, and had associated with it hours of great labour and anxiety—not the labour of the hand, but of the mind; not in the selection of goods and materials, highly valuable as that duty is, but in the selection of men who had brains and capacity equal to the demands made upon them in their various positions. I soon learnt an important lesson, which I commend to every responsible man here, viz., that if I could not forgive a little—in other words, if I could not pass by or be blind and deaf to many actions and sayings of unkind or thoughtless people, not alone those in our employ—I should be worried and disabled for the duties required from a director in a large manufacturing and mercantile house, and so I set myself to cultivate self-restraint, and a more difficult task no man can enter upon, who has a will and any force of character. Unkind words or deeds, unhappy manners of those around you or those you have to do business with, are of frequent occurrence. Many men are so constituted that they cannot help it; they are angular and left-handed in everything they do. It is nothing extraordinary. Many are afflicted with the power and disposition of seeing and doing things the wrong way. Friends, we must be firm and kind in our conduct, and remember it is not possible to run all men in the same mould. Your exercise of this power of forbearance and forgiveness is very largely the measure of your own capacity and manliness. I don't forget it is equally incumbent upon the employer to be thoughtful, considerate, and helpful as it is upon the employed, but the demands upon the men in the various positions are very different. In no case, however, can the necessity for courtesy and consideration be abrogated. As I said a few days ago, this is a period of great pleasure to me, but not unmixed with other feelings. I have entered upon my sixty-seventh year, and though I feel to-day as well in health as ever I did, yet the fact is there, that however buoyant I may be in spirit, however conscious I may feel as to my powers to assist in the administration of this gigantic concern, and with your co-operation to help it on to a greater position than it has yet attained—I say, notwithstanding all this, the machinery of the constitution has been in active service for a long period, and in the later years has been worked at a higher speed, greater pressure being required; and though many surrounding facilities can and have been obtained to sustain the machine, yet we have each only so much power and so much phosphorus in the brain, and when these are exhausted the work must cease. How near that period is I cannot by any means find out. It cannot be very far off. I cannot sit down without making kind reference to my late colleague—your late leading director, Mr. Hoggan—under whose guidance, joined with his best and truest of friends, Mr. Carnelley, assisted by Mr. Mitchener, your concern has grown to a magnificent house. The buyers and managers in the offices, and the travellers, including our recently-appointed director, Mr. Dunford, have done their work nobly. You have good men through the house; you have a magnificent field for operation—a grand name attached to it, and ample means. These are powers which can and will make the firm take a higher position; and, while doing so, we wish success to all our neighbours who are equally industrious and equally worthy. I conclude by again thanking you very sincerely for your great kindness.

After a vote of thanks to the chairman the company adjourned to the Grand Hall to listen to the concert of the Longford Musical Society.

Chapter XVII.

TRAVELLERS' AND FOREIGN AGENTS' PRESENTATION.

AT a special meeting of the Travellers and Foreign Agents, Mr. Kemp being in the chair, the following address was read and presented to Mr. Reuben Spencer:—

"To REUBEN SPENCER, Esquire, J.P.
"Rylands & Sons, Limited, Manchester.

"DEAR SIR,—We the Representatives and Agents of the Home and Foreign Department of Rylands & Sons, Limited, Manchester, most gladly present you our hearty good wishes on the occasion of your Jubilee. We desire to express our satisfaction for the robust health with which you have been enabled, almost without a break, to discharge the duties of your position for the long term of fifty years. We congratulate you upon your brilliantly successful career, and admire your many remarkable qualities.

"While we confirm all that has been said in your favour by other sections of the Company, we desire especially to refer to the ability you have always displayed in making plain the various difficulties which environ the path of a traveller, and the kindly interest you have always evinced in their welfare, also the generous consideration and sound judgment you have displayed in giving preference to the rising young men of the house who have aspired to become travellers, rather than yield to applications from without.

"We would respectfully record our appreciation of the confidence you repose in us as a body, leaving much to our discretion and relying upon our probity; the firm but kindly wisdom of your decisions, whereby we cannot fail to recognise the high regard in which you hold the paramount interests of the firm.

"We have watched with pride the remarkable success which has attended your efforts, in conjunction with the Directorate, in promoting the Company's business, and especially in the extension of the Export Trade, resulting in developments which are the surprise and wonder of the mercantile community, and far exceeding the highest expectation of the most sanguine. We trust you may long be spared to occupy the honourable post you now so ably fill, and continue to contribute to the successful guidance of the multifarious and important affairs of the colossal business of Rylands & Sons, Limited.

"We ask your acceptance of this illuminated Address and of the Album containing portraits of the Travellers, and, on Mrs. Spencer's behalf, of the accompanying Silver Dessert Service, which we trust will serve as a lasting memento of the respect and high esteem in which you are held by the Representatives and Agents of the firm.

"For the Representatives and Agents of Rylands & Sons, Limited, Manchester :—

"JAMES KEMP.
"H. H. HARTSHORNE.
"THOS. SCHOLES.
"DAVID THOMAS.
"SAMUEL COLLIER.
"GEO. FLANNAGAN, Hon. Sec."

Mr. Reuben Spencer made the following reply:

"Mr. Kemp, Mr. Collier, Mr. Hartshorne, Mr. Flannagan, Mr. Thomas, and Mr. Scholes, you have been appointed to represent the honoured band of travellers and agents in arranging for the dinner which you propose to give a short time hence; the writing of the address, the preparation of the album, and the purchase of the magnificent silver dessert service, which, for richness of design, beauty, and value, is worthy of you and far in excess of my expectation, I am sure the buyers, chief clerks, salesmen, and others, who have before joined together in making presents to Mrs. Spencer and myself, will excuse me saying I think you have acted kindly in thus holding a special meeting. Gentlemen, I cannot refrain from the expression of my high appreciation of your valuable services in assisting to raise this grand concern; whilst I think of you I cannot but recall our old friends, Mr. Search, Mr. Williams, Mr. Criddle, Mr. Mellor, Mr. Donald, and Mr. Kirrelly, to whom I shall make further reference; they were men of the highest mark, and, like you, contributed largely to raise the house to its present proud position. I notice that you six gentlemen forming the committee represent a period of close upon two hundred years' service with the firm, and it reminds me of another gathering of a similar kind when four of us sitting together represented a total service of two hundred and twenty-five years.

"Gentlemen, these are remarkable facts and figures, perfectly unique and probably unmatched in any commercial house; and, what is more, we none of us say or feel we are fossilised or exhausted either in body, mind, or heart; we have life and energy yet to do yeoman service. We feel bound to you and to the old house; it is not the bond of the merely mercenary selfish man, but a bond of friendship, and of united cheerful attachment to each other, inspired by one desire to seek the prosperity of the concern which includes and involves the good of each and all. You are quite justified, and it is pleasing to the directors to see you recognise and appreciate the principle which has guided us in our management of the firm's business, viz:—to watch for the young man who shows capacity, industry, and integrity, and place him in a situation of an improving character. I might ask whence came our buyers, our chiefs in the various departments, and conspicuously our travellers? They came from the body of men who were of our own training, and if there is a class of men amongst us to whom I have given special thought and consideration, it has been our travellers. My brother directors and I feel no small measure of pride in raising such men—nay, I will rather say in being able to give free scope to men who have shown such spirit, ability, and indomitable will. You call me a friend, and so I have tried to be to you all, however unfortunate my manner of exhibiting the feeling has sometimes been. Feltham says, 'The noblest part of a friend is an honest boldness in the notifying of errors. He that tells me of a fault aiming at my good, I must think him wise and faithful: wise in spying that which I see not, faithful in a plain admonishment not tainted with flattery.'

"Gentlemen, in each instance where, through the kindness and generosity of my friends in various parts of our business, it has been determined in some practical and kindly form to recognise my jubilee, I have endeavoured to say a few words appropriate to the occasion. In addressing you, allow me to say you are undoubtedly representative men; and in a far higher sense than is generally attached to that word, the graphic form adopted in our grammar-books as to value—viz., good, better, and best—is most appropriate to you.

"We have a large staff all good, not a few better, and a number of whom I may say that the word best does not convey the full breadth of my feeling. They are men whose social and commercial influence is very great, and it arises from various causes. In some, ripened experience combined with energy of character and good-will; in others, with indomitable energy, enthusiasm, and courage; in others, with persuasive power and with tact that ever succeeds; and with all a manly bearing and a conviction that they know their business and are the right men with the right firm, with whom it is a pleasure to be associated. And here I must, by your permission, refer to the six representatives I had in my mind when addressing the audience before me a few days ago at Belle Vue. Mr. Search, who was accustomed to wear a blue coat of the finest texture and value, with gold buttons and a frilled shirt, every inch an English gentleman, highly esteemed and successful. Mr. Criddle, a good and true man of the highest stamp of a commercial traveller, whose integrity of character and purpose could never be questioned, esteemed by all his customers, and also respected by his employers. Mr. Williams, who was so well known and respected in South Wales that it was a common remark to hear, when his address was asked for at any time, ' Oh, Mr. W. Williams—South Wales is quite sufficient, he is known everywhere,' and certainly there was some truth in the statement. He was widely known and respected, and eminently successful. Then came the able, cultured, and thorough gentleman, Mr. John Mellor, a man who was admired by all in the house, and by all the friends on the ground on which he was accustomed to travel. His influence was marked, and hundreds of traders of his day and of this day willingly accorded to him their thanks for his advice and direction, alike in their business and social relations. He was a man of high character and of great industry. He was appointed to the position of Director of the Company, from which he retired some years ago, and there is not a man left who does not wish him to be spared for many years to enjoy the rest he has well earned. I make similar remarks as to the character of Mr. Donald and Mr. Kirrelly. I cannot but feel that at a date—somewhat distant I hope—many meetings for different objects will be held amongst our successors, when pleasant reference will be made to not a few of those whose names appear on this address, and whose portraits I am proud to possess in this album.

"There are few positions in which an intelligent,

observant man, with a healthy constitution, can find greater scope for his energy and capacity, and in which he can exercise a more helpful and generally beneficial influence, than a commercial traveller representing a good house. He can secure and enjoy at the same time the confidence and respect of his customers and of the house he represents. If ever there was a band of capable and true men, who watched the interest and supported the character and dignity of any large commercial firm, it surely is the band of men who occupy the position of travellers and representatives in Rylands & Sons, Limited. Amongst you there is as much variety of character as it is possible to find among a hundred leading men in any place or community. Gentlemen, I gladly and willingly admit you have much to do with the destiny of the house; but, happily for you, you have not to bear the burden and responsibility of those who have to deal with the official and financial duties of the house, or with the manufacturing portion of the business in which are engaged such a great staff of servants and such a large portion of the capital of the Company.

"You can and do give the directors very valuable assistance in many ways, and as Chairman of the Company I know I am voicing the feeling of my co-directors when I say we appreciate your services most highly, and are pleased to have this opportunity of expressing our esteem and sense of obligation to you. I claim to speak with authority on this matter, I have known every one of you from the commencement of your services in the firm. Speaking for myself and my wife, I thank you most heartily for your magnificent present as an expression of your good feeling on the attainment of my jubilee.

"I hope that we all may be spared some time to work in support of the grand old firm we have so long served, and that we may see greater things achieved than have yet been accomplished."

Chapter XVIII.

REUBEN SPENCER, ESQ., J.P.

THE annals of public and commercial life in Manchester are singularly rich in examples of genuine devotion to the duties of citizenship on the part of men who have achieved personal distinction and eminence of position, not by any fortuitous combination of lucky circumstances, but by the union of natural talents and abilities with steady perseverance and unceasing industry. The records of such men, wherever they are found, furnish abundant proof of the incontestable fact that those who of necessity labour most arduously in the advancement of their own affairs are frequently the first to consecrate their brief moments of leisure to the public service. Having regard to Manchester in particular, where hard work has always been recognised as the *sine quâ non* of material prosperity, it would be impossible to name a city whose leading men in various spheres of activity have displayed a more striking *esprit de corps* as citizens, or manifested greater unanimity in their desire for the welfare of the community, and in their efforts to secure the same. This highly commendable spirit has been particularly conspicuous among the great merchants of the city—a fraternity of which the subject of our present sketch is one of the most prominent, energetic, and respected members.

Though not a Lancastrian by birth, it has been the fortune of Mr. Reuben Spencer to become peculiarly and specially identified with Manchester. His name is, indeed, widely familiar in commercial circles generally, and especially in connection with the textile trade; yet it is in the city of Manchester that the effect of his life-work has been most noticeable and noteworthy, and it is by the people of this city that he himself is now honoured in an exceptional degree. Coming here in the days of his youth from the hillsides of a neighbouring county, associating himself with the greatest house in the Manchester trade, becoming gradually a recognised leader in the commercial and social advancement of the place, and taking a part of ever-increasing activity in the work of many of its principal institutions, there is hardly a department of life in Manchester in which Mr. Reuben Spencer has not figured prominently, or in which he has not proved himself in some measure a pioneer of progress.

Mr. Spencer is a native of Derbyshire, and was born at Belper on September 18th, 1830. At an early age he came to Manchester, after receiving a useful education at his native place, and forthwith entered upon a career of commercial activity which has now extended over half a century. His first post in Manchester was in an accountant's office, where he remained twelve months. At the expiration of that period, by the assistance of his then employer and an old friend, he obtained a situation in the great firm of Rylands & Sons, with which he has ever since remained associated. In the service of that famous house, young Reuben Spencer was speedily brought under the influence of that very remarkable man, the late John Rylands, who will go down to history as one of the greatest commercial administrators of any age, and as the founder and organiser of the most gigantic of the many vast businesses that have grown up and flourished in Lancashire.

As an indication of Mr. Spencer's regard for, and high opinion of his former chief, we may here recall a few words on that point which he used not long ago in an address to young men :—" I do not hesitate to say that, next to the powerful influence of my mother, I received my most healthy and manly inspiration from Mr. Rylands. He was a capable man, an able administrator, and by his side I learnt much that has been of great—I had almost said invaluable—service to me in my commercial life." The address from which the above sentences are taken was in many respects a notable one, embodying thoughts and comments well calculated to impress an audience of young men with the duties and labours of life all before them. In the course of its delivery, Mr. Spencer took occasion to speak of the institutions connected with the house of Rylands (one of them a tribute to the memory of the deceased founder of the firm), and as his remarks thereupon afford a glimpse of what is being done, and has been done, to promote the general well-being of the whole staff of this great concern, they may appropriately be quoted here, particularly as they reveal the depth of Mr. Spencer's personal interest in the institutions to which he refers, and which he has himself done so much to foster. These are his words:—"However much I may feel interested in the various educational and charitable institutions of our city, none can command my sympathy so much as the two great and useful societies, or institutions we have in connection with the firm of Rylands & Sons, Limited, viz., the Rylands Packers' and Porters' Benevolent Fund, specially confined to them), and the Rylands Memorial Club, which embraces the buyers, travellers, salesmen, and clerks, together with the leading men engaged in our seventeen factories and works. The objects of this club are almost as far-reaching in their influence as are the various branches of trade represented by the members. I had the pleasure of presiding at the first meeting and making a statement as to the objects of the club, the number of which has, however, since been extended. It was founded to do honour to the memory of the late John Rylands, whom we all admired as a noble example of business capacity. The club embraces the following branches: A 'thrift fund,' to which all can make monthly contributions, securing, in addition to five per cent. interest allowed, a considerable bonus, which is added every five years, thus comprehending in some measure the purposes of a life insurance, and also of an important provision for old age. Then we have a fire brigade for the protection of our own property, which is thoroughly equipped, and would be found of great service if called to duty. We have also an orchestral society, brass and string bands, chess, cricket, football, and rowing clubs, and last, but not least, a special fund, supported by the company, to meet any exceptional case of distress or trouble occurring to any of the members, which fund is under the care and direction of the directors."

Many years elapsed between the eventful day upon which Mr. Spencer first entered the house of Rylands & Sons in a subordinate capacity and that upon which he ultimately became a partner in this colossal concern; but those who know the man and his methods will require no special assurance of the fact that the whole of that long intervening period was employed by him in the conscientious discharge of every duty that fell to his lot, and in the steadfast pursuit of a line of action which could hardly lead to any other result than his own continuous promotion and the equally constant advancement of the firm's interests. It may be unhesitatingly averred that, next to its late head, no one has contributed more largely to the prosperity of the house of Rylands & Sons than Mr. Reuben Spencer, and his admission to the partnership upwards of twenty years ago was a practical recognition of and tribute to his great services to the firm. Ultimately, on the formation of the limited liability company by which this great business (or rather group of businesses) is now controlled, Mr. Spencer became a director, and he continues to discharge the functions of this post with undiminished energy and assiduity.

To a man of Mr. Spencer's character and capacity invitations to participate in the active labour of municipal life are inevitable, and we shall presently see that his strong sense of public duty has constrained him to take up a vast amount of work which a less public-spirited man would willingly avoid. There are, however, limits to the human capacity for exertion, and Mr. Spencer has been obliged in some cases to acknowledge this. Frequently he has been asked to accept positions which the manifold nature of his other engagements would absolutely preclude his filling. Requests to contest Manchester for the office of City Councillor, and to "stand" for various parliamentary constituencies, have been forthcoming on more than one occasion, but all these he has been compelled to decline, because he felt that he could not discharge the duties they involved and at the same time maintain the efficiency of his work in other connections, particularly in relation to the great commercial concern over which he exercises exceptional influence.

This is not the place to enter into descriptive details concerning the industrial and mercantile operations of Rylands & Sons, Limited, but when we consider the unparalleled magnitude to which this company's undertakings have now attained in their particular line—utilising a share and debenture capital of £2,900,000, with land, buildings, and machinery valued at over £1,000,000 sterling, and employing upwards of twelve thousand hands, the majority of whom work in some seventeen mills, factories, and warehouses—it must be admitted that the administrative routine of such a concern calls for a display of energy that might well constitute a good and sufficient excuse for any member of the Board for complete abstention from any public work whatever. For the latter, however, Mr. Spencer manages to find a surprisingly large amount of time, and this is due to the fact that he neglects no opportunity which even the briefest spell of leisure affords. Whatever time he contrives by systematic methods to snatch from the daily round of business labour, he apportions with strict fairness among a variety of public avocations which, in themselves, strikingly attest his versatile powers. Perhaps the first place is occupied by his functions as a magistrate, which he discharges with scrupulous care and diligence; and the rest of his work, in connection with a multitude of commercial, educational, and philanthropic institutions, assuredly affords occupation for many more days and hours of leisure than the majority of men would care to resign even to the most deserving causes.

There are few institutions and movements of recent years bearing a close relationship to life in Manchester that have not engaged in some useful and beneficial degree the personal interest of Mr. Reuben Spencer. Perhaps in none of these notable undertakings have his services been more conspicuous or fruitful in good results than in the great work of rousing public interest in the Manchester Ship Canal, and securing support for that gigantic work, fraught with such great consequences, and pregnant with so many possibilities for the welfare of the vast population inhabiting the district through which its course has at last been triumphantly carried.

We might fill several pages in recounting the occasions upon which Mr. Spencer has publicly championed the cause of the Ship Canal, and reports of the many earnest and trenchant speeches he has delivered in its favour from time to time would fill many more. All his work in this connection was characterised by the utmost zeal for the object in view, as well as by a manifest confidence in its ultimate success which, we doubt not, frequently inspired a similar confidence in others. He even went so far as to organise and act as treasurer of a committee formed in the warehouse of Rylands & Son's to arrange and carry out a scheme for raising funds to assist the Ship Canal enterprise, and the result of which was a very valuable addition to the financial resources of the great undertaking. . Future years will doubtless justify the hopes and realise the anticipations of those who have laboured in behalf of the Manchester Ship Canal, now auspiciously completed and fairly in working order ; and when the services of its promoters and supporters come to be reckoned up and appraised, those rendered by Mr. Reuben Spencer will certainly not stand lowest in value nor least in estimation. The support accorded by him to the Ship Canal in the early stages of its eventful career was especially useful as coming at a critical period, and he received the express thanks of the Provisional Committee for his evidence in favour of the Canal Bill when it came before the Select Committee of the House of Lords in 1885. He also participated in the congratulations conveyed by the Provisional Committee of the Ship Canal to the various societies and gentlemen who assisted in the promotion of the very successful demonstration held in favour of the Canal at Pomona Gardens in June, 1884, and we may add he is the President of the " Ship Canal Shareholders Association."

Everybody who has studied the home trade of

Manchester and its progress in recent years will be familiar with the nature and importance of Mr. Reuben Spencer's work in this connection; and will remember how largely instrumental he was in securing the due recognition of this great branch of the city's trade by the Manchester Chamber of Commerce. The ultimate result of the efforts made by himself and colleagues in this direction was the appointment by the Chamber of Commerce, in November, 1890, of a new committee, styled the "Home Trade Sectional Committee." Of this committee Mr. Spencer was unanimously elected Chairman, a post he continues to hold, and he has since been chosen Vice-President of the Chamber, from which fact may be inferred his probable occupancy of the chair, if matters take the usual course in the coming year. Again, he has been most active and zealous in promoting the growth and influence of the Manchester Guardian and Trade Protection Society, of which he is Vice-President, and which now numbers upwards of five thousand members.

Among the many charitable and benevolent institutions in which Mr. Spencer has taken an active interest, perhaps the most important is the Warehousemen and Clerks' Schools, of which he is a Vice-President, and the Warehousemen and Clerks' Provident Association, of which he is President, a great organisation, with no less than four thousand five hundred members; President of the Manchester and

Salford Penitentiary; Trustee of Nicholl's Hospital, and of the Dental Hospital; a member of the Committee of the Lancashire Independent College; and an active participant in the support and administration of many miscellaneous charities. Formerly Mr. Spencer was President of the Commercial Travellers' Association, but was obliged to retire from that office in consequence of excess of other work. The public press of Manchester and Lancashire, for a good many years past, has placed on permanent record many other phases of his activity as a citizen animated by a constant and lively desire for the promotion of civic and social welfare. Time and again he has presided at meetings convened to further movements tending in this direction, and his many speeches and letters to the press abound with thoughtful and practical suggestions, such as might be expected from one who has repeatedly proved himself a sound man of business, a shrewd student of events, and a sympathetic observer of life in the varied aspects in which it presents itself in such a city as Manchester, and in such a district as that of the county of Lancaster in general.

Politically, Mr. Spencer is a Liberal, and has undertaken a fair share of labour and responsibility in furthering the principles he holds. In religion he adheres to the Congregational body, and in various capacities connected with that denomination, such as college committee work and church and school building associations, he has rendered services none the less valuable because they have been perfectly unostentatious.

Finally, in the sphere of literary labour Mr. Spencer has been more prominent than most business men, and has shown himself a thoughtful and lucid writer upon topics which enlist his interest and sympathy. To many his most important work is that entitled the "Home Trade of Manchester," a volume dedicated to the members of the Rylands Memorial Club, and originally published under the *nom de plume* of "Home Trader." However much Mr. Spencer might have wished to preserve his *incognito* in this matter, the authorship of the book soon became an open secret, and in subsequent editions (of which there have been several) his name duly appears upon the title-page. The work is a really masterly disquisition upon a subject which is particularly congenial to its author, and upon which he is entitled to discourse with authority. It contains a great store of historical and mercantile lore, equally accurate and instructive, and adds to this a fund of anecdotal interest in the shape of personal reminiscences extending over the lengthy period covered by Mr. Spencer's personal association with Manchester. Such a volume is a distinct acquisition to the literature of our national commerce, and can be read with pleasure and profit by anyone in the least degree interested in the important subject of which it treats.

Another notable work from Mr. Spencer's pen is the volume entitled, "To Young Men going out into Life," in which the author endeavours, with marked success, to place at the disposal of young men entering upon the responsible work of life the results of long experience and close observation, and to assist his readers with knowledge which could only be acquired in such a position as that which he himself has filled. In these pages many valuable hints are conveyed to young business men concerning the application of their capital and the advantageous employment of their powers and resources generally, and these hints are followed up with others intended to assist the reader at a more mature period of life in the further development of his business, whether it be wholesale or retail, home or export. Our author likewise seeks to show that commercial life, properly lived, has higher and nobler aims than the mere acquisition of wealth; and, consistently with the salient features of his own exemplary career, he points the way to many paths of usefulness that open themselves to the business man gifted with intelligence, energy, and the desire to benefit his fellows and leave the world a little better than he found it. The whole tone of the book is healthy. It breathes a spirit of encouragement from first to last, and it will prove helpful and instructive to every young man who reads it in thoughtful earnest. For those embarking in the textile trade it may stand as a textbook, not alone of the broad principles of successful commerce, but also of the many lesser details which must engage the serious attention of the young merchant who hopes to prosper.

Mr. Spencer also produced for the use of the Manchester trade an excellent "Telegraphic Code," and a very comprehensive "Ready Reckoner." We imagine that his moments of recreation must be few and far between. Nevertheless, he thinks (and we agree with him) that every man should have a hobby, and his own has been the collecting of ancient and modern coins, medals, &c., in silver, gold, and bronze. Of these numismatic treasures he has amassed a goodly and representative collection, which he has now, with characteristic generosity, presented to the Museum of the Victoria University, Manchester.

Though he has entered upon his sixty-seventh year, Mr. Reuben Spencer preserves unimpaired the physical and mental vigour that has served him so well throughout his exceptionally active and useful career. Of his personality we need not speak. The kindly face and genial manner are familiar to scores of friends who will join us in wishing him many more years of health and strength in which to sustain his part, and continue his services as an upright and enterprising merchant and a public-spirited citizen.

The records of many brilliant individualities will come under the consideration of future historians of

Manchester; few of these, it may safely be asserted, will command a larger amount of attention than that of Mr. Reuben Spencer; and none, we are confident, will prove richer in that encouragement to others which is always embodied, to some extent, in distinguished and successful careers.

www.ingramcontent.com/pod-product-compliance
Lightning Source LLC
Chambersburg PA
CBHW031740230426
43669CB00007B/424